BEYOND THE MONUMENTS IN WASHINGTON, DC

D1427665

CONTENTS

WELCOME TO WASHINGTON, DC

From the moment I spied the Washington Monument out the plane window, as we cruised over the green lawn of the National Mall, I was captivated. It was 2014, and I was freshly arrived from Australia.

In this city, I learned on the ground, America's past is chiseled in stone, from the wise words of Abraham Lincoln on the walls of the Lincoln Memorial to the impressive figure of Dr. Martin Luther King Jr. towering over the Tidal Basin nearby. And I felt the legacies of the country's forebears in the colossal neoclassical buildings, along that expansive Mall, around the Tidal Basin, and in corners of the Smithsonian museums. For DC's past is indeed a powerful one.

But there's a lot more to DC than Big Things. It took me time to explore the rest of the city, and to discover that the streets and corners beyond that monument-studded Mall are just as fascinating. What I've found, especially in recent years, are wonderful neighborhoods in the midst of minor revolutions—and even some neighborhoods built from scratch. In the short time I've been here, District Wharf, Navy Yard, and Union Market District have sprung up virtually overnight, to the delight of younger locals especially. Across the city, chef-driven restaurants—from multicultural eateries to artisanal ice cream parlors—have taken off, as have sleek cocktail bars, edgy speakeasies, and craft breweries, not to mention retro movie houses and avant-garde theaters. And I have come to see that the true foundation of the city is, of course, its people: DC's active LGBTQIA+ scene, for instance, as well as a large student population, immigrants from around the globe, and international politicos—all communities that add to the city's monumental reputation.

To be clear: I wasn't born in the United States. I didn't go to high school here. And I still can't tell a half-smoke from a hot dog. But I have made Washington, DC, my part-time home for a decade—time enough for me to tackle the city with gusto, without ever taking it for granted. I hope my insider-outsider perspective and my passion for the city will direct you to places beyond the monuments that reflect DC's extraordinary history and culture—alongside its contemporary soul.

ABOUT WASHINGTON, DC

Like a prim and proper great aunt, Washington, DC, maintains a façade that's a little prudish. Yet behind the veneer lies the odd scandal—and a saucier, more vibrant personality than first meets the eye.

The Federal District—later the District of Columbia—was founded in 1790 to be America's permanent capital (Philadelphia had been the first, temporary one), built from the ground up and home to all three branches of the US government. As part of his gig as the nation's first president, George Washington marked the bounds of the new district. He first outlined a square, 10 miles (16km) on each side and rotated 45 degrees: a diamond when viewed on a map. Divided by the Potomac River, the district was half in the state of Maryland and half in the state of Virginia—that is, until disgruntled Virginians went and ruined the shape by reclaiming their patch. Many quip that it now looks like a diamond with a bite out of its southwest side. In the central portion of the diamond, Frenchman Pierre L'Enfant designed a distinctive street plan, still in use today. With the Capitol at the center, he divided the diamond into quadrants (Northeast, Southeast, Southwest, Northwest), then drew a grid of lettered (east–west) and numbered (north–south) streets, plus wide diagonal boulevards named for states, all punctuated by parklike traffic circles.

The street plan was barely filled in when the city was nearly destroyed during the War of 1812, against Great Britain. Decades later, after the Civil War, formerly enslaved people settled here, and gradually the city grew, first expanding around Capitol Hill and Lafayette Square, home to the White House, and then encompassing Georgetown, a nearby port town on the Potomac River. In 1957, DC became the first majority Black city in the United States.

Another key turning point came on April 4, 1968, with the assassination of Dr. Martin Luther King Jr. The ensuing protests and riots destroyed buildings and businesses in several central neighborhoods. In recent decades, these areas have begun to revive—though at the same time, the Black population has dwindled, losing its majority in DC in 2011.

About

ABOUT WASHINGTON, DC

One chronic sore spot in the city: From the start, the Constitution specified that the District would fall directly under federal control—but that has meant that, unlike residents of the 50 states, the people who live in the District have no one to speak for their interests in Congress. There is a movement to grant the District statehood, and the current DC license plate reads, echoing the slogan of the American Revolution, "End Taxation Without Representation."

Through it all, the National Mall has grown into a tree-lined strip of lawn that stretches some 2.2 miles (3.5km) between the Lincoln Memorial and the Capitol, marked at the center by the white obelisk of the Washington Monument. The area is still a work in progress, thanks to the dynamic Smithsonian collections as well as newer museums, such as the National Museum of African American History & Culture, which opened in 2016.

As a kind of front yard for the nation, the Mall is also a highly symbolic and recognizable site for politics, protests, and celebrations. It's where King gave his "I Have a Dream" speech in 1963, indeed where any rally seeking the country's attention convenes (including the one that ended in the attack on the Capitol in January 2021), and where thousands swarm for festivities, such as Independence Day fireworks against the backdrop of the Monument.

On a day-to-day basis, most of DC's 670,000 residents enjoy hanging out in the District's smaller neighborhoods that are home to great eateries, rooftop bars, and cool-cat cafés. Plus local stores, indie theaters, and lush parks (vast Rock Creek Park runs north to south through the city). Or they head to the city's new urban developments—such as District Wharf, in a reclaimed section of the Washington Channel, and Navy Yard, on the Anacostia River. And, of course, many of the 4.7 million people in the Maryland and Virginia suburbs head to the city to enjoy these too.

What makes the District different from anywhere else is the energy that swirls around the nation's most iconic buildings, its actual halls of power. To understand DC, you'll want to see both the great American monuments and the city life beyond them.

WASHINGTON, DC

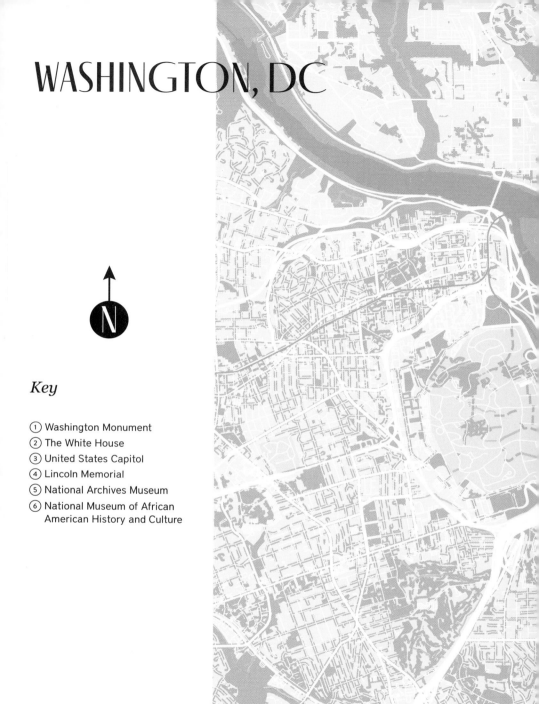

N

Key

1. Washington Monument
2. The White House
3. United States Capitol
4. Lincoln Memorial
5. National Archives Museum
6. National Museum of African
   American History and Culture

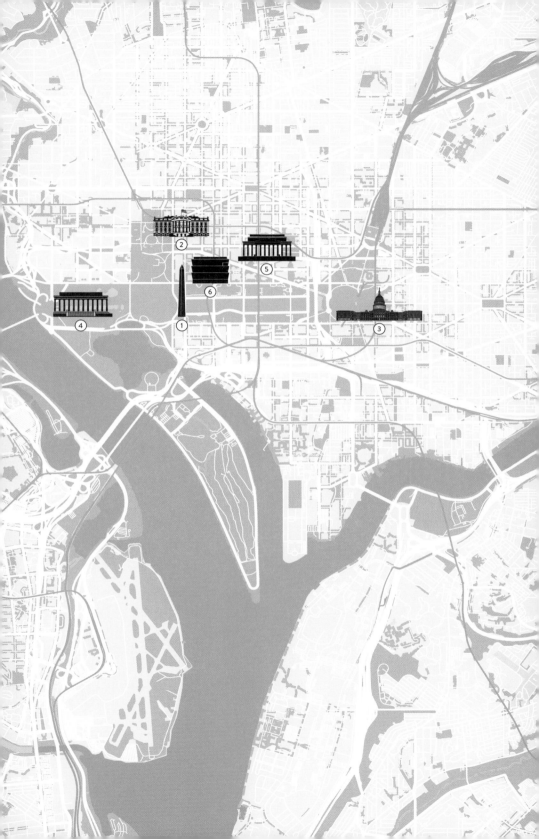

NEIGHBORHOOD INDEX

NEIGHBORHOOD INDEX

NOTABLE NEIGHBORHOODS

DC residents use the city's quadrants (Northeast, Southeast, etc.) as broad brushstrokes, but the city is unofficially divided into smaller neighborhoods. This book covers the areas and commercial corridors that locals consider "central," as well as several neighborhoods beyond, including a few of the city's liveliest new redeveloped areas. We start at the Mall, DC's monumental heart, and explore roughly clockwise; the listings in this book follow this order.

NATIONAL MALL

In 1791, Pierre L'Enfant envisioned a "grand avenue" with trees and embassies extending west from the Capitol, but this was not implemented, and the land became a patchwork of parks and gardens. His idea was revived in 1902, when the McMillan Commission (a panel that included landscape architect Frederick Law Olmsted Jr., son of the designer of NYC's Central Park) took on a new urban plan. This specified a lawn between the Capitol and the Washington Monument—the original National Mall.

These days, to all but the most finicky, "the Mall" means the whole 2.2 miles (3.5km) of grass that extends west past the Monument to the Lincoln and Jefferson memorials. The massive lawn—with the towering central obelisk of the Monument, a landmark from all over the city—is one of the most symbolic and familiar sites in the country, featured in news reports, movies, and TV shows. For locals, the Mall is a daily playground; you might see touch rugby and Ultimate games here, and joggers running around its perimeter. Visitors come for the eleven Smithsonian museums and numerous memorials.

NOTABLE NEIGHBORHOODS

PENN QUARTER AND DOWNTOWN

East of the White House and north of Pennsylvania Avenue, Penn Quarter is where, in the economic and population boom after World War I, architects literally went to town, designing neoclassical civic temples that survive today as government offices and museums. But after residents began moving to the suburbs in the 1950s, the thriving neighborhood basically died; on passing through the area on his 1961 inauguration parade, President Kennedy is said to have commented on its run-down state. In the 1990s, a redevelopment initiative built the MCI Center—now the Capital One Arena, home to the Washington Wizards (basketball) and the Capitals (hockey). These days, Penn Quarter and the rest of the downtown area (including, but not limited to, Chinatown, Federal Triangle, Vernon Square, and up to Logan Circle) is lively, with destination entertainment and dining—such as China Chilcano (see p.106) and The Hamilton (see p.108). And some of those neoclassical temples house two of DC's best free museums, the National Portrait Gallery (see p.167) and the National Archives Museum (see p.157).

GEORGETOWN

Historic Georgetown is among the city's greenest and chicest districts. It's known for its eponymous university, beautiful mansions, and the commercial strips along M Street (mostly chain stores) and Wisconsin Avenue (more independent shops). At the time the District was drawn, Georgetown had already been a busy port town on the Potomac River for 40 years; it wasn't incorporated into the city of Washington until 1871. Famous residents include George Washington's granddaughter Martha (see Tudor Place, p.185); John and Jackie Kennedy (John proposed at Martin's Tavern; see p.115); actor Elizabeth Taylor; French-cooking doyenne Julia Child; and Pulitzer Prize–winning author Herman Wouk. The somewhat recent resurrection of industrial buildings and alleys around the Chesapeake & Ohio Canal, home to backstreet gems such as Baked & Wired (see p.47) and Grace Street Coffee (see p.49), has added some contemporary polish.

DUPONT CIRCLE AND FOGGY BOTTOM

For the first-time visitor, Dupont Circle can be a little confusing. Yes, it's a literal giant traffic circle, in the middle of which is an attractive lawn, benches, and a Beaux-Arts fountain (1921) that honors a Civil War rear admiral and features three classical nudes. But the name also refers to the neighborhood along the spoke streets that extend from the circle: New Hampshire, Connecticut, and

NOTABLE NEIGHBORHOODS

Massachusetts Avenues (this last includes the lovely strip of buildings known as Embassy Row). A hodgepodge of commerce includes bars, take-out joints, and eateries of all standards; this is also DC's longest-established gayborhood.

South of Dupont Circle and east to the White House, you'll find Foggy Bottom (locals don't blink twice at its quaint name). Its remaining historic mansions reflect its status as one of DC's oldest neighborhoods. These days, it's home to The George Washington University (and its hospital), and a handy metro stop for Georgetown, a 15-minute walk. Much of the area is modern apartments and offices, though it harbors a few appealing coffee and food options.

ADAMS MORGAN

A bit like the university students who are drawn here by cheap drinks, a party atmosphere, and lack of pretension, Adams Morgan fluctuates between being downright grungy and über-smart. Easily accessible from downtown by bus, the area spreads up the hill beyond U Street, and much of the action is on the unshaded commercial strips of Florida Avenue, Columbia Road, and 18th Street. These form a triangle of hedonism (some might say debauchery, especially during happy hour) that draws social folks of all kinds, beyond the student crowd. These streets are also where laid-back cafés abut rooftop bars, and mom-and-pop Ethiopian restaurants stand adjacent to more upmarket eateries. (Forgot to make dinner reservations? Try Adams Morgan, as lots of restaurants here don't bother with them.) The narrow residential streets are lined with tightly packed row houses that compete for space with the neighborhood trees. Head a couple of blocks off the commercial strips, and the area is very pretty.

14TH STREET

As recently as 2014, old-timers would warn me away from 14th Street. The stretch between U Street and Logan Circle had a reputation as a hotbed of DC's more colorful activities and businesses, whether you wanted to buy a used car, a woman's services, or some illegal substances. Then smart residential apartments sprouted seemingly overnight, along with the requisite high-end supermarkets Trader Joe's and Whole Foods. The rapid gentrification has been controversial, but now 14th Street is the opposite of a no-go zone: a bustling entertainment magnet for cool cats of all ages, as well as the LGBTQIA+ community, with an explosion of restaurants, some with street dining, from Michelin-starred eateries to holes-in-the wall, plus decent bars and nightclubs.

NOTABLE NEIGHBORHOODS

SHAW AND U STREET

A center of Black cultural and intellectual life since the 1860s, Shaw is home to Howard University and the Howard Theatre, which used to be part of a larger "Black Broadway" entertainment scene along nearby U Street.

Today, after a decades-long slide in the late 20th century and a recent surge in gentrification, Shaw is, for better and worse, one of DC's most energetic and youthful districts, with some of the city's cooler restaurants and bars. It lacks the greenery of other areas, and the 19th-century row houses and industrial buildings still exude a slightly gritty vibe. Don't expect a continuous strip of neon lights. Instead, seek out more discreet eateries down alleys (Tiger Fork, see p.138), on rooftops (El Techo, see p.84), or in converted warehouses (Right Proper Brewing Company, see p.91).

H STREET AND NOMA

The 1.5-mile (2.5km) strip of H Street east of Union Station was one of DC's earliest big commercial hubs (the city's first Sears Roebuck department store was here). But the street lost its gloss after WWII, and more so after the 1968 riots. In the 2010s, it was finally revived from grungy decline, with some key chain stores and a free streetcar (dcstreetcar.com), like the one that ran until 1962. While the area can be a tad soulless by day, it's lively in the evening, when an eclectic range of restaurants—such as hip-vegan Fancy Radish (p.139) and faux-Swiss-lodge Stable (p.141)—open their doors, and quirky bars start to rattle their cocktail shakers. Some patches of the strip are still a little gritty, though, so stay alert at night.

The west end of the H Street strip, between First and Fourth Streets, falls within NoMa, the newly revitalized residential area *no*rth of *Ma*ssachusetts, where a hip, youngish professional crowd fills its many new buildings.

UNION MARKET DISTRICT

This roughly four-by-four grid of streets was once a key hub for food wholesalers, anchored by the public Union Market. That market closed in the 1980s, and businesses began to move out, leaving empty warehouses and loading docks. Since a redevelopment scheme started in 2012, the identity of this tiny area has been almost completely reforged, with upscale eateries, arty cafés, and faux-grunge bars—though the area hasn't lost its industrial character, thanks to a few tenacious wholesale dealers.

NOTABLE NEIGHBORHOODS

A modern food hall fills Union Market (see p.147), with purveyors like the District Fishwife (see p.144). In the surrounding streets, you'll find, among other things, a distillery (Cotton & Reed, see p.94), a community-focused café (The Village DC, see p.61), and another small market, La Cosecha (see p.201), all Latin-American-themed. Union Market District epitomizes gentrification, yet it still manages to be a center of community and creative enterprises. It's a fun place to wander, particularly on the weekends when crowds create a buzzy ambiance.

CAPITOL HILL

Nowhere represents DC more than the hill on which stands the magnificent domed US Capitol, flanked by the Senate and House buildings, the Library of Congress, and the Supreme Court. East of these landmarks is DC's most historical residential neighborhood, also called Capitol Hill, where, in the early 1800s, taverns and boarding houses provided beds for members of Congress. Today, gorgeous leafy streets are lined with row houses, Federal-style town houses, and posh mansions. Most of the cafés and bars can be found around buzzy Eastern Market (built in 1873) and along 7th Street and historic Barracks Row (8th Street SE), once home to all the diverse workers of the naval yard due south, on the Anacostia River.

WATERFRONT DC

Two of DC's newest reincarnations are on the water: District Wharf (see p.169), a former maritime center and fish market, and Navy Yard, which was a busy shipbuilding and munitions port in the 19th century.

Both precincts received multibillion-dollar overhauls that transformed them into thriving destinations with polished restaurants, residential apartment blocks, and entertainment venues. Weekends are busy, as visitors of all ages come to eat and browse.

District Wharf sits due south of the Mall, on the Washington Canal, off the Potomac River. Navy Yard is only 1.5 miles (2.4km) away, on the Anacostia River south of Capitol Hill. The walk between the two takes about 30 minutes, but unfortunately the route is not along the waterways.

Neighborhoods

CONSTITUTIONAL CAPERS

FULL-DAY ITINERARY

This route takes in some of the landmarks around the National Mall that are most linked to American history and governance—with a special focus on the power of words. It constitutes a solid day of sightseeing, though the biggest sights come first, so you can stop at lunchtime if you prefer. Be sure to schedule tours and timed tickets online beforehand.

8:30AM After reserving for the day's first tour, arrive early at the ① **US Capitol** (see p.165) to go through airport-style security; bring only a small bag, and no food or drink, including water. Enter into the visitor center, which occupies an entire 580,000 square feet (54,000 sq m) underground on the building's eastern side.

Your visit starts in Emancipation Hall, dedicated to the enslaved workers who helped build the Capitol. At the center is the original plaster model for *Freedom Triumphant in War and Peace*, the colossal bronze figure that tops the Capitol dome. After a short video on Congress and its role in American democracy, you'll join a docent for a 45-minute tour through several key spaces in the building: the Rotunda, the "crypt" below, and a hall of statues gifted by the states. Depending on crowds, you might also get to visit the small chamber that first served as the Senate.

After your tour, explore the rest of Emancipation Hall, along with the Exhibition Hall, which houses modern displays about Congress, the Capitol, and how the three branches of government interact.

10:00AM From the Capitol visitor center, walk through an underground tunnel to the ② **Library of Congress Thomas Jefferson Building** (see p.155). Alternatively, you can head there aboveground (a 5-minute stroll east across 1st Street).

The Jefferson Building is the most beautiful of the national library's three buildings. Wander through the magnificent gilded Italian Renaissance–style hall, gaze up at the masterful dome in the main reading room, check out the replica of Jefferson's library, and admire some very, very old books. At the time of research no tours were running (check on arrival), but knowledgeable docents are on hand to answer any questions.

12:00PM If you're up for a 30-minute walk, head off the Mall: north up 1st Street, northwest on Constitution Ave, and north again on 7th Street. Here you'll find ③ **China Chilcano** (see p.106), good if you want to dine in.

But if the weather is good for a picnic, you can opt for (4) **Bindaas Bowls** (sister eatery to **Bindaas**; see p.103) for takeout, then make the short walk back south on 7th Street to Constitution Avenue and the National Gallery of Art's sculpture garden and enjoy an alfresco meal surrounded by famous statues.

1:30PM A massive neoclassical building just north of the sculpture garden, across Constitution Avenue, the (5) **National Archives Museum** (see p.157) displays America's fundamental documents: the Declaration of Independence, the Constitution, and the Bill of Rights. Allow additional time to peruse the absorbing public vaults, full of interactive displays of documents, photos, and recordings.

3PM Outside the National Archives, head north on 9th Street then left (northwest) on Pennsylvania Avenue. On the left just before the corner of 12th Street is the Waldorf Astoria DC Hotel, a landmark since it opened as DC's main post office in 1899. It was later redeveloped as a hotel by Donald Trump, who sold the lease after he left office; it rebranded in 2022. The building's tall clock tower (9am–3:45pm daily) is run by the National Parks Service; enter on 12th Street, across from the Federal Triangle Metro station, to take the glass elevator to the top for excellent views.

3:30PM Walk one block farther on Pennsylvania Avenue and turn right (north) on 13th Street. Ten minutes straight on, at K Street, is (6) **Planet Word** (see p.178), an interactive museum dedicated to the world's languages that will have you not only reading, but also shouting and singing.

5PM Time to analyze all those words you've absorbed—perhaps with the aid of a strong drink. Either head for (7) **Jane Jane** (see p.79), a 20-minute walk north, at 14th Street and R Street, and from there to a plethora of restaurants on the same strip. Or walk half a mile east on K Street and jog north on 7th Street to (8) **Morris American Bar** (see p.88), then finish up with a Georgian meal at (9) **Supra** (see p.137), a few blocks back northwest, at M Street and 11th Street.

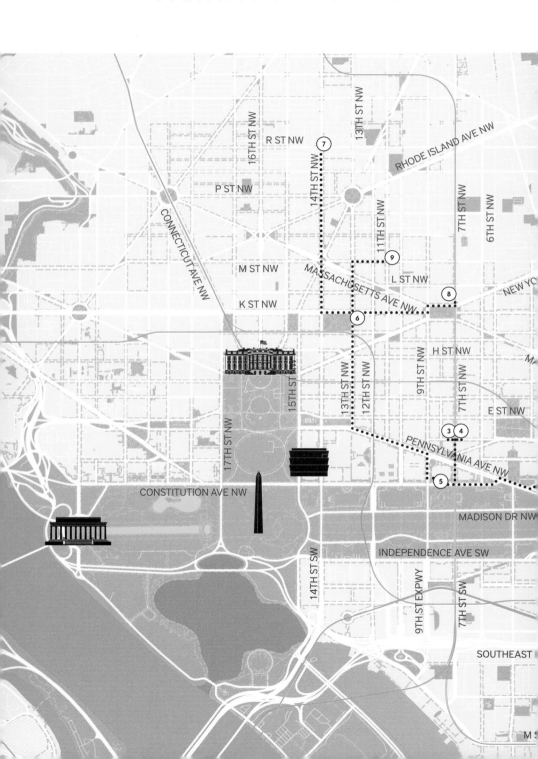

T NW

NTH CAPITOL ST NE

H ST NE

TTS AVE NW

2ND ST NE

6TH ST NE

MARYLAND AVE NE

CONSTITUTION AVE NW

1ST S   SE

①

EAST CAPITOL ST SE

②

NTH CAROLINA AVE SE

INDEPENDENCE AVE SE

11TH ST SE

2ND ST SE

8TH ST SE

PENNSYLVANIA AVE SE

STH CAPITOL ST SE

SOUTHEAST FWY

M ST SE

GEORGETOWN JAUNT

FULL-DAY ITINERARY

*This architecturally distinct neighborhood—a port town before DC existed—
is also one of the city's most elite and lush. Its tree-shaded streets, opulent
mansions, colorful cottages, and walled gardens are probably home to a
ghost—or a few. This full-day itinerary is heavy on historic homes and
gardens, with breaks for coffee and shopping—but if you opt out of one
property or the shops, you can enjoy it in half a day.*

10AM Kick off the day with a quality coffee and cupcake (yes, quality
enough for breakfast!) from ① **Baked & Wired** (see p.47). Munch away while
overlooking the C&O Canal, once a major transport thoroughfare.

10:30AM Head one block north on Thomas Jefferson Street. Across M Street
and a little left is Old Stone House, built around 1765 and considered the
oldest building in the District, predating the American Revolution. Continue
west on M Street to Wisconsin Avenue and turn right. Do a dry run window-
shopping at the boutiques (you'll loop back later when they're all open).
At the corner of N Street is the Georgetown classic ② **Martin's Tavern**
(see p.115), where, in Booth 3, then-Senator John F. Kennedy proposed to
Jacqueline Bouvier.

11:00AM Turn left (west) on N Street: Jackie and JFK lived at 3307, a
Federal-style house, before leaving for the White House. Backtrack to 33rd
Street and turn left (north), and after three blocks, right (east) at Volta Place.
At the corner with Wisconsin Avenue is the pretty Georgetown Lutheran
Church, the oldest Lutheran congregation in the country, established in 1769.
Jog north on Wisconsin Avenue to the next right (east), Q Street; go two
blocks and turn left (north) on 31st Street. Midblock on the left is the entry to
⑤ **Tudor Place** (see p.185), the historic home (completed in 1816) of Martha
Custis Peter, George Washington's granddaughter. The house remained in
her family until the 1980s; now it's a museum with quirky antiques, including
some of George's personal items; allow some time to wander through the
beautiful gardens.

12:00PM Head north on 31st Street to R Street and ramble through
⑤ **Dumbarton Oaks Gardens** (see p.181), and not to be confused with
Dumbarton House on Q Street), a gorgeous 16-acre estate that's especially
pretty in springtime. The mansion displays a collection of Byzantine and
pre-Columbian art, a library, and the jewel, El Greco's *Visitation*.

1PM Continue east on R Street to Oak Hill Cemetery, a 22-acre historic graveyard alongside a Gothic Revival chapel designed by James Renwick (best known for the Smithsonian Castle, as well as St. Patrick's Cathedral in New York City). Willie Lincoln, the son of Abraham Lincoln who died of typhoid at 11, is buried here. Opposite the cemetery, 2920 R Street NW was the home of Katharine Graham, former publisher of the *Washington Post*, depicted by Meryl Streep in the 2017 movie *The Post*.

2PM It's definitely time for a picnic lunch: Head east on R Street to 28th Street and turn right (south) to reach ⑥ **Stachowski's** (see p.118), a butcher shop, deli, and grocery renowned for its cured meats—but it caters to non-meat-eaters too. Pick up a gourmet sandwich and head east on P Street to Rose Park. If you're done for the day, continue east on P Street for 15 minutes to reach Dupont Circle.

3PM From the south side of Rose Park, head west along O Street then one block south on 27th Street to Dumbarton, where you'll pass First Baptist Church, Georgetown, founded in 1862 by the Reverend Sandy Alexander, a former enslaved person. Two blocks west, at 29th Street, is Mount Zion United Methodist Church (1816), the oldest Black congregation in the area.

3:30PM Double back to First Baptist Church and continue south on 27th Street two blocks to Olive Street; the first house, the appropriately butter-yellow 2706, was home base for American culinary legend Julia Child from 1948 to 1959.

Continue west on Olive Street to 30th Street and turn left (south). The next block is M Street, Georgetown's main commercial strip, where you can turn right to browse and shop. Just south of M Street on Thomas Jefferson Street, enjoy a predinner drink and vistas at ⑦ **The Rooftop at the Graham** (see p.70).

5PM Take Thomas Jefferson Street south all the way to Georgetown Waterfront Park, located in a development known as the Washington Harbour, lined with smart eateries. In winter, a small ice rink lures novice skaters. From here, soak up the views of the Potomac River as well as the Kennedy Center and Francis Scott Key Bridge, named after the Georgetown lawyer who penned "The Star-Spangled Banner." For dinner, Georgetown's options are only average. You could loop back to Martin's Tavern for passable pub fare, or grab a cab to Dupont Circle or 14th Street for more choices.

BLACK BROADWAY AND BEYOND

HALF-DAY ITINERARY

Following the Civil War, U Street grew into a prosperous hub of Black American life. In the 1940s, when countless jazz artists performed here, it was dubbed Black Broadway. In 1968, though, this area was ground zero for the riots following the assassination of Martin Luther King. This itinerary will plunge you into the strip's rich, and sometimes challenging, African American history; informative plaques along the route provide further detail.

11AM Start with a quality coffee at ① **The Coffee Bar** (see p.52), a neighborhood café with a pretty outdoor patio.

11:30AM Wander north along 12th Street to the Thurgood Marshall Center, an Italian Renaissance–style building that housed the first African American YMCA in the US (1835).

Turn right (east) at T Street, then make a soft left (northeast) onto Vermont Avenue. Ahead on the right is the African American Civil War Memorial Museum, dedicated to the more than 200,000 Black soldiers who fought in the Civil War.

Continue on Vermont to U Street and turn left (west). Down on the left, note the mural of Mr. William and Mrs. Winifred Lee on the alley side of Lee's Flower Shop, which has been selling blooms since 1945.

Cross 11th Street to Industrial Bank, one of the country's first Black-owned banks (1913). At 1200 U Street, the former True Reformer Building (1903) was designed, financed, and constructed by Black Americans. Duke Ellington played his first paid performance here.

12:00PM Farther down U Street, on the north side, is DC institution ② **Ben's Chili Bowl** (see p.131), which opened in 1958 and operated all through the 1968 riots. Performers such as Miles Davis and Nat King Cole used to hang out here. Grab a half-smoke, a DC-area food curiosity—it's like a hot dog with attitude.

A mural on the side of the building showcases famous Black Americans such as Barack and Michelle Obama, Prince, Harriet Tubman, DC natives Taraji P. Henson and Wale (whose video "Chillin'" was shot at Ben's), and Roberta Flack, who attended nearby Howard University.

12:30PM Next door to Ben's, the neoclassical Lincoln Theatre opened in 1922, closed after the 1968 riots, and in 1994 reopened as a performing arts center.

Walk another block and a half west on U Street and turn left on 14th. At the corner of V Street is ③ **Busboys and Poets** (see p.126), a bookstore-café; have a hearty lunch of shrimp and grits or a blackened salmon salad.

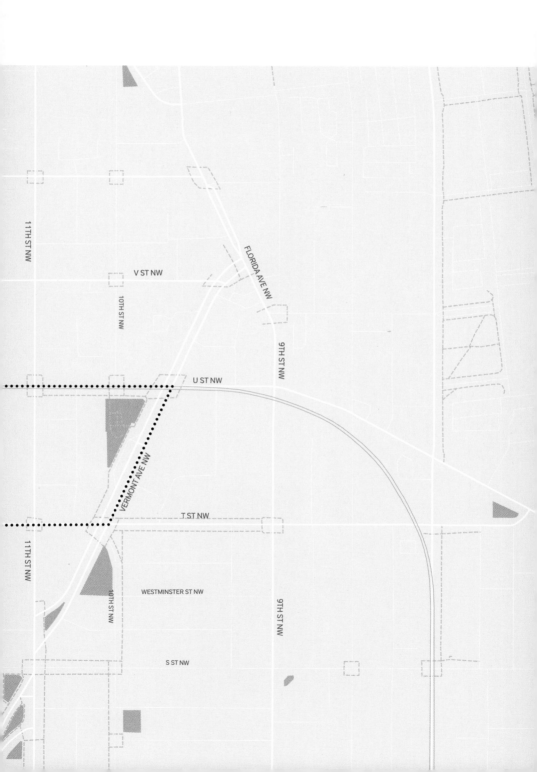

BRUNCH BREAKS

To outsiders, the stereotypical meal in DC is the power lunch. But in my opinion, the city's real specialty is a long, relaxed weekend brunch—and nowhere, but nowhere, does it better than Washington, DC. The scene has only become more popular over the years as the city has grown less formal. Locals work hard, and weekends are the time to let their hair down with friends. But who needs an excuse?

Brunch service, usually with a menu of egg dishes and sweet-savory combos like chicken and waffles, typically runs on weekends from 11am to 4pm (to some foreigners, for whom brunch is earlier, this is more of an all-day breakfast). Typically you'll get bottomless mimosas—or some other fresh and lightly alcoholic drink—where your glass is filled and refilled. More often than not, brunch means large groups of friends and raucous laughter (quiet nooks with the newspaper are hard to find). Of the many restaurants that do weekend brunches, these are some of my faves.

The Greenhouse

Private, quiet, and old-fashioned taste of historic DC.

1200 16th Street NW

W

www.jeffersondc.com

Mon 7am–10:30am & 11am–2pm

Tues–Fri 7am–10:30am, 11am–2pm & 5:30–9pm

Sat 8am–1:30pm & 5:30–9pm

Sun 8am–1:30pm

USD

$$$

If you want to immerse yourself in DC elegance with a touch of '80s power brunch, head for the restaurant at The Jefferson hotel. The Greenhouse is indeed a bright spot filled with flowers and lush plants. But the glory goes to the dramatic vaulted skylight. Part of the original 1923 apartment complex, it was covered in concrete during World War II. Only in 2007, during a major renovation of the hotel, was it rediscovered and restored.

The decor skews traditional—black-and-white checkerboard floor, white tablecloths—and this, plus the older clientele of politicians and embassy folk, makes for a somewhat hushed ambience, a nice alternative to louder party brunches.

The menu too is classic and somewhat seasonal: eggs Benedict, blueberry French toast, Chesapeake smoked salmon, and eggs baked in wee cast-iron skillets.

It's an experience to linger over, as it's not cheap. But it will set you up for an afternoon of sightseeing (the White House is four blocks away). Reserve ahead.

Piccolina da Centrolina

Airy, gourmet Italian café in the posh City Center complex.

---

963 Palmer Alley NW

W

piccolinadc.com

Mon—Sun 8am—9pm

USD

$$

The sister of Centrolina, a popular, smart Italian restaurant just across the alley, Piccolina continues the Mediterranean theme in a sunny, contemporary space.

In the wood-fired oven, chef Amy Brandwein and her team conjure up a wonderful range of treats: Everything from panini and pizza to salmon skewers release a delicious smoky flavor; the giardino panino, a thin bread filled with roasted vegetables, is especially good. More typical brunch treats include house-made granola and a puffy egg on brioche. The menu standout, the 10-layer eggplant parmigiana, is perfect for any meal. Of the range of fresh pastries on show, the bomboloni (custard pastries) are at the top of my list. Couple it with excellent coffee, and you'll be set for a few hours.

Residents

Extra-friendly neighborhood hangout with eclectic décor, cocktails, and dishes.

This friendly place wears its heart in its name, which refers to its group of co-owners, all residents of DC. Their passion for community, color, and idiosyncratic style permeates this charming restaurant-café-bar.

Its small indoor space and larger front patio are decorated with a lovely mix of textured cushions and throws. And plants feature strongly here, so you might also find a (plastic) frond in your highly acclaimed cocktail. Winners include the espresso martini and Mexican coffee (with a kick of mezcal), but the mocktails—some seasonal, as well as a pink-hued coconut water—look as beautiful as their alcohol-fueled counterparts.

Weekend brunch doesn't get much better than Turkish-style baked eggs on pita with garlic yogurt, or the outstanding French toast bites with dulce de leche. My only gripe is the steep price for coffee. By night the buzz gets louder as a thirtysomething crowd flocks for drinks and food. I like the bistro filet, but others swear by the burgers. Don't miss the Madagascar vanilla soft-serve ice cream.

📍

1306 18th Street NW

W

residentsdc.com

🕑

Tues–Thurs 4–11pm

Fri 5pm–12am

Sat 11am–12am

Sun 11am–10pm

USD

$$

Kafe Leopold

European-owned, reliable Georgetown café-restaurant.

3315 Cady's Alley NW

W

instagram.com/
kafeleopold

Mon–Sun 8am–10pm

USD

$$

Tucked away in a refurbished lane parallel to M Street, the long-established Kafe Leopold is a magnet for ladies who lunch. That said, brunch also draws families, tourists, and local businessfolk. The patio, with a small fountain in the center, is especially pleasant during warmer weather. The owner is Austrian, and the theme is definitely European.

Frühstück–breakfast–is good value for Georgetown: for instance, two eggs any style with grilled rosemary ham and toast, for around $12. Muesli and a decent fruit plate provide healthy options. The European pastries are an unexpected pleasure (I mean, who doesn't love a rich, chocolatey Sachertorte?). Beyond brunch, there's great salads such as tuna Niçoise and the signature dish, Leopold's Schnitzel.

Enter via M Street between 33rd and 34th Streets: Duck through the archway and head down a flight of stairs.

Lutèce

Journey through France, with some twists and many local ingredients.

1522 Wisconsin Avenue NW

W

lutecedc.com

Mon & Thurs 5–9pm
Fri 5–10pm
Sat 11am–3pm & 5–10pm
Sun 11am–3pm & 5–9pm

USD

$$$

This charming locale, with a brick-walled dining room and a romantic bar area, is the nearest thing DC has to a Parisian bistro. Ingredients are sourced from the DMV (that's local shorthand for DC, Maryland, and Virginia), which means a frequently changing menu and a fresh, simple approach to preparing delicious delights.

Evening meals may stretch the budget, but there's good value in the weekend brunches, when the kitchen whips up a lovely smoked salmon brioche with crème fraiche, an avocado tartine, and yes, even a cheeseburger—with caramelized onion and miso for extra savor, and Dijon mustard for a French kick. The brunch cocktails—Bloody Marys and mimosas—are all-American.

Terrace seating in fine weather makes you feel like you're on the Champs-Élysées (well, if you squint).

The Fainting Goat

Hip, low-key bar serving gourmet hangover fare.

1330 U Street NW

W

faintinggoatdc.com

Tues–Thurs 5–11pm
Fri & Sat 11am–4:30pm
(kitchen closes at
3:30pm), 5pm–12am
(kitchen closes at 10pm)
Sun 11am–4:30pm &
5–11pm (kitchen closes
at 10pm)

USD

$$

This casual and welcoming spot oozes industrial style: exposed brick and sparkly chandeliers. Sure, it's cool (even down to its Instagram hashtag, #feedthegoat), but what I love is its creative approach. On the menu, brunch dishes read as typical—burgers, a croque monsieur, French toast—but arrive at your table with a lot more flair. The burger, for example, is a 7-ounce beef patty with tomato jam and pickles, both house-made. And sweet tooths need look no further than the brioche French toast, which is more like a custardy bread pudding, with lush rum-caramel cream.

Seal the good-value deal with bottomless mimosas, Bloody Marys, and even sangria. Caffeine addicts note: There's drip coffee only, though sourced from a reputable, local company.

Another, non-brunch draw is the popular trivia night, Wednesdays at 7pm.

Nina May

Gorgeous neighborhood eatery that shows why brunch is such a big deal in DC.

1337 11th Street NW

W

ninamaydc.com

Tues–Thurs 5–10pm
Fri 5–11pm
Sat 10am–3pm & 5–11pm
Sun 10am–3pm & 5–10pm

USD

$$$

From the moment you enter this friendly spot, hidden away on a leafy residential street, you'll feel at home. Seating options include a lovely outdoor pergola, a small open terrace, and a light-filled interior. The dishes and changing menu are welcome relief from some of the stock-standard offerings elsewhere. The seasonal and local ingredients are sourced from farms within 150 miles (241km) of DC.

For a relaxed weekend brunch, consider the Chef's Choice, four dishes shared among two people. The à la carte options may include a perfectly done omelet (runnier in the center) or polenta with trumpet mushrooms. The standout is the orange ricotta pancakes with peanut-butter cream, always on the menu, regardless of season (there'd be an uproar if they were removed).

Get there early if you haven't reserved ahead.

Unconventional Diner

American comfort food with flair.

1207 9th Street NW

W

unconventionaldiner.com

Mon–Sun 9am–10pm

USD

$$

This is one of the few places in DC that serves a brunch menu daily until 4pm, which is great for late starters. The massive, minimalist-chic space has seats at a long counter, as well as oodles of tables—basically a trendy diner, but with plenty of room and without the sticky-Formica factor.

The reliable menu will fill any hole with hearty dishes like chicken and waffles (the specialty), Caribbean-spiced shrimp and grits, and stacks of buttermilk pancakes. A healthier (and very good) option is the "everything lox" plate, a poached egg enveloped in lox and garnished with capers and more. Decent cocktails start at around $14.

My only gripe? A cappuccino here costs even more than at a cutting-edge coffee bar. And it can get noisy (especially when happy hour starts at 3:30pm); sensitive souls should opt for an outside table.

Ambar

Balkan eatery with DC's best unlimited brunch deal.

---

523 8th Street SE

W

ambarrestaurant.com

Mon–Thurs 12pm–3:30pm
& 4–10pm
Fri 12pm–3:30pm &
4–11pm
Sat 10am–3:30pm &
4:30–11pm
Sun 10am–3:30pm &
4:30–10pm

USD

$$

Spread over three levels in a Barracks Row building, this Balkan-themed place makes ordering easy: Pay one price (in the case of brunch, $35), and get as much as you like. This means you can try the likes of cheese pies, beet tzatziki, pork-belly-stuffed cabbage, kebabs—whatever is on its ever-changing menu. One constant, the baked pita bread, is great.

Service is efficient, and the staff, many of whom are from Serbia, know their stuff. But the usual all-you-can-eat caveats apply: Don't get carried away, as it's easy to order...until (burp!) you can't eat any more. And take your time, because the food is fresh and delicious—organic, local produce stars in many dishes—so you don't want to just wolf it down.

An extra $9 gets you unlimited drinks as well: juices or Bloody Marys or mimosas.

Crazy Aunt Helen's

*American-style brunch in a bright and happy spot
where everybody's welcome.*

This vibrant Capitol Hill favorite, decked out in a delightfully zany way with
the help of the owner's creative friend, Miss Pixie (known for her eponymous
knickknack shop, see p.194), features a hodgepodge of bright-pink trim and
lime-green banquette seating and tables set with mismatched dishes and
silverware. It's a refreshing change from some of DC's sleeker "hipster" haunts
and sets an "everybody's welcome" tone where it's easy to settle in.

Home-style American comfort food is the focus: nothing too fancy,
but generous portions of eggs and ham with grits or potatoes. All produce
is from the DMV area, as are the beers and the spirits for the cocktails (try
Crazy Aunt Helen's reviving Salty Dog). A carb kick comes in the form of
the biscuit with strawberries, ice cream, and whipped cream, just as the
welcoming owner's grandmother used to make.

A light well down one side lets the sun in, and bright-pink vintage
tables and chairs fill a pretty front terrace too. Don't miss a brunch here if
drag queen Tara Hoot is performing (usually monthly). A hoot indeed: Even
families flock to see her.

📍	🕑	**USD**
713 8th Street SE	Wed–Fri 11:30am–3pm	$$
	& 5–9pm	
W	Sat & Sun 10am–3pm	
crazyaunthelens.com	& 5–9pm	

COFFEE CAUCUS

Let's be frank: DC's coffee scene ain't that of Portland or Seattle or New York. Yet. But it's definitely brewing, while catering to all tastes, whether you want a single-origin brew or some soy-and-strawberry-syrup-minus-any-hint-of-a-bean beverage. The usual chains are here, but of course more intriguing caffeinated pleasures can be found in more indie-style neighborhood hangouts that are serious about flavor, brewing methods, and even latte art: cute kitten-head-on-foam, coming right up.

My favorite spots in the current bean scene include The Coffee Bar (see p. 52), for its quality beans and pleasant outdoor patio, Grace Street Coffee (see p. 49), for its consistency, Baked & Wired (see p. 47; and its sister café, A Baked Joint; see p. 57), for fabulous variety and latte art, and Café Unido (see p. 59), for its Panamanian flair. (Unfortunately, paper cups are common, whether "for here" or "to go," but extra credit to all of these cafés for using ceramic cups, my personal preference.) Many of these cafés serve light meals, including good salads and sandwiches. These won't break the bank, coming in at the $ to $$ range.

Dolcezza at the Hirshhorn

Where coffee is an art form. Literally.

Independence Avenue SW
and 7th Street SW

dolcezzagelato.com

Sun–Thurs 8am–11pm
Fri & Sat 8am–12am

Opened in 2018, photographer and architect Hiroshi Sugimoto's redesign of the lobby of the Hirshhorn Museum (see p.154) is a kind of vast functional sculpture—including a striking long metal coffee bar.

In keeping with the high design, the coffee is very good. Beans are roasted locally, and the baristas whip up quality creations, from cappuccino to nitro cold brews. Dolcezza (which has five other locations in town) is also known for its small-batch seasonal gelato—which, perhaps to protect the museum's collection from sticky fingers, is sold outside in the courtyard, and only in summer. Year-round, though, you can get fresh pastries.

Sugimoto also designed the chairs with their curving backs—echoing the modernist building's cylindrical shape—and two remarkable tables made from the roots of a 700-year-old Japanese nutmeg tree. Settle in with your treats, and you're part of the artwork.

Bluestone Lane

Sunny café with a touch of Australia.

1100 23rd Street NW

W

bluestonelane.com

Mon–Sun 7:30am–5pm

This casual-chic, Australian-style spot used to be among my faves—I was finally able to get a proper flat white in DC. And then the chain (based in New York City, cofounded by an ex-Aussie rules footballer) expanded further, and the coffee has become a bit hit or miss, depending on the barista.

Nevertheless, what saves this particular branch is its glorious setting next to the West End Library, with a sun-drenched interior and a pretty patio. The Instagram-perfect design pops with serene touches of green—dark leafy wallpaper, mint and neutral timber, sea-foam tiles—and every seat is a winner, whether in the well-cushioned banquettes or the tables by the floor-to-ceiling windows.

The excellent menu includes brunch-ish eggs and delicious, ultra-healthy salads—and of course, something Australians claim to have invented (though, as an Aussie, I can hardly understand why): avocado toast, on the menu here under its Melbourne moniker, avocado smash. And this version *is* very good.

For Five Coffee Roasters

Quality coffee, healthy lunch bites, and great pastries.

2000 L Street NW

forfivecoffee.com

Mon–Sun 7am–6pm

This branch of For Five, a small chain based in New York City, is set up like a cocktail bar for coffee lovers, where the milk and cold brew is on tap, and you can prop yourself on a bar seat and chat to the many students and office workers who escape to this airy refuge.

I most often get a good and simple cortado, but the most popular drink here is the Five, a rich blend of drip brew, espresso, chocolate ganache, and steamed half-and-half, garnished with a twist of orange peel. It might sound gimmicky, but it uses fundamentally great coffee, such as various excellent African blends and mild roasts.

And unlike at many coffee bars, the food is no afterthought. Wholesome breakfasts and delicious lunch items use fresh seasonal ingredients: a wild-mushroom omelet, for example, as well as a tuna poke bowl and a BLAT sandwich. It's all worth the walk into Foggy Bottom.

Baked & Wired

DC's best cupcakes and superior brews.

1052 Thomas Jefferson Street NW

W

bakedandwired.com

Mon–Sun 8am–4pm

Located by the C&O Canal, Baked & Wired serves some of the city's most reliably good coffee. Unfortunately, the store is rather cramped, with a slightly grungy rear section, so the well-executed coffees, from cappuccinos to pour-overs, are best enjoyed as takeout—unless you can nab one of the seats out front on the sidewalk, in which case you'll also enjoy a proper ceramic cup. (Otherwise, grab a public bench on the canal.)

Along with your brew, pick from the selection of baked goods, including whimsically-named cupcakes for which Baked & Wired is justifiably DC-famous. It's hard to pass up the Razmanian Devil (lemon cake with raspberry jam), but my favorite is the Chocolate Doom. All are made with impeccably good ingredients.

Weekends get busy, and don't bother bringing a laptop, even on weekdays: There is no Wi-Fi.

Compass Coffee

Strong ethics guide this coffee from the tree to your cup.

1351 Wisconsin Avenue NW

W

compasscoffee.com

Mon–Fri 6am–6pm
Sat & Sun 7am–7pm

Orienting toward Compass Coffee is easy: Just look for the building's retro signage, a big red neon "Georgetown," a legacy of the building's past life as a cinema. Inside, the space is airy and modern, usually busy with students and freelancers on their laptops.

The coffee, though, is the real mission: The blends and single-origin beans (some of which are organic) are all sustainably grown, ethically harvested, and fairly traded. They appeal more to American tastes, with dark roasts and flavored brews, though lighter roasts are also pulled from the sleek bank of espresso levers. Specialty seasonal roasts are available too, along the lines of springtime Cherry Blossom. A selection of croissants, scones, and muffins seals the deal.

Be sure to request a ceramic mug; the default is (in contrast with its bean ethics) a paper cup.

Grace Street Coffee

Great coffee, bikes, and a whole(some) lot more.

3210 Grace Street NW

W

gracestcoffee.com

Mon–Thurs 8am–6pm
Fri & Sat 8am–7pm
Sun 8am–5pm

A bike shop adjoins this industrial-chic café with concrete floors, minimalist décor, and long windows. During the week you order on entry, then settle in to one of the 10 or so tables, while on weekends there's a server to take your order at the table.

The baristas serve up some of DC's best coffee, made from responsibly sourced Ethiopian beans. Cappuccinos, pour-overs, and siphon cold brews are a hit, and in summer, the zesty lemon matcha will cool you down. If you're hungry, pick from a basic but very good selection of all-day breakfasts, from smoked salmon and salads to granola and yogurt. Note, though, that weekends between 10am and noon are marked by spandex-clad bikers crowding in, peloton-style, for a caffeine fix after their morning rides.

Potter's House

Coffee, bakery snacks, and books for people with a conscience.

1658 Columbia Road NW

W

pottershousedc.org

Mon–Sun 8:30am–2:30pm

One of DC's first coffeehouses, opened in 1960, this nonprofit café in Adams Morgan is a pleasant surprise. It's set around a modern bookstore, with titles covering justice and equity, cultural studies, and spiritual traditions.

As the name—and some of the book titles—suggest, the place has Christian roots, but it is in no way a place for proselytizing. Rather, its community philosophy is about paying it forward: Your coffee purchase funds the organization, and—as a discreet notice on the counter suggests—it's easy to make an extra donation for meals for those in need. The Potter's House especially strives to support people who have been displaced by gentrification.

It's a vibrant, diverse space, and its long experience in the world of coffee shows: Brews are very good, and if you add a simple huevos rancheros or fresh pastry, you've got yourself a tasty breakfast or lunch that's also socially responsible.

Tryst

DC's self-appointed "community living room" lives up to its name.

📍

2459 18th Street NW

W

trystdc.com

🕐

Mon–Sun 7am–9pm

Tryst celebrates difference and diversity, even in its aesthetics: a thrown-together, vintage-shop vibe of mismatched furniture, silverware, and squishy sofas. Many younger locals gather here over coffee, alcoholic beverages, and craft brews while taking advantage of the Wi-Fi.

But if you're after DC's absolute best cup of joe, perhaps this isn't the place for you. While the full gamut of specialty coffees is on the menu, they're only okay, in my humble brew-lovin' opinion. But hey, each cup does come with animal crackers on the side.

Still, the café's atmosphere and welcoming vibe make up for any blip in caffeine standards. The extensive sandwich menu, served all day, won't break the bank. Excellent sweet treats (I can't resist the brownie and the carrot cake) and reasonably priced cocktails might mean you settle in for longer than intended.

The Coffee Bar

*Relaxing neighborhood
joint with friendly,
experienced baristas.*

1201 S Street NW

W

thecoffeebardc.com

Mon–Fri 7am–5pm
Sat & Sun 8am–6pm

Known just as TCB to its regulars, the Coffee Bar has been open since 2012 in a pretty, historic building from 1880. The casual, welcoming ambience—with a large sofa inside, lots of reclaimed wood and other upcycled materials, roomy patio tables, and good Wi-Fi—attracts everyone from young freelance workers to local families to dog walkers. (Dogs are permitted at the outdoor seating.)

On the weekends, you might encounter a line, but don't worry—the baristas make it move fast, even with a varied menu of "on tap" cold brew and a selection of pour-over options with beans from specialty US-based roasters. All the same, less-crowded weekdays are preferable if you want to linger and mingle. Unfortunately, there's no food other than some baked goods.

TCB is an easy walk from 14th Street or south of U Street, and a short detour from the self-guided civil-rights history walk that is signed around the area.

Colada Shop

Taste Little Havana in the heart of DC.

1405 T Street NW

W

coladashop.com

Coffee Mon–Sun 8am–9pm

Café Wed 3–9pm

Thurs & Fri 3–10pm

Sat 11am–10pm

Sun 11am–9pm

This hospitable Cuban-style coffee spot conjures Miami with vivid colors and outdoor counter service on sunny days. Walk right up and get a very good cortadito, that distinctly Cuban coffee topped with sweet coffee foam. And while you're at it, get a guava-and-cheese pastelito or a heartier empanada (there's always a seasonal flavor).

The founder, a young coffee lover from the Dominican Republic, had a vision of a social café: conversation, cocktails, and Cuban food. That's on display especially in the upstairs space, where the rooftop patio shifts into a vibrant bar at happy hour (Monday to Friday, 3pm to 6pm), and tasty seasonal cocktails are served for less than $10.

Colada Shop has expanded into a local mini-chain, with house-branded products. To my taste, it's a bit of a retail gimmick, but the original outlet, on the corner of 14th and T Streets, is delightful nonetheless.

Slipstream

Excellent coffee beans and blends with a semi-scientific approach.

When this café opened in Logan Circle in 2014, it felt like a laboratory, with lots of glass beakers, serious precision, and deep analysis of origin and methodology. I'm not saying the baristas are less rigorous these days (the coffee is *very* good), but the approach has lightened up, and the menu now includes some syrupy novelties that won't thrill coffee purists. That said, they clearly know their acids and overtones of chocolate and berry, as reflected in their bean selections, both single origins and blends.

Floor-to-ceiling windows provide the front seats with a view of the street, but the windowless rear section is less appealing (it attracts laptop workers looking for less distraction). Still, if you can nab a table, stay for an excellent breakfast, such as a granola bowl, an avocado toast, or the tasty breakfast sandwich.

This is the original Slipstream location. Of the two others, the newer one, at 82 I Street SE, in a quieter area of Navy Yard, is worth a visit for its more pleasant, spacious feel and blond-wood trim. It's also a quick 15-minute walk south of the Library of Congress.

1333 14th Street NW

slipstreamdc.com

Mon–Thurs 7am–10pm
Fri 7am–11:30pm
Sat 8am–11:30pm
Sun 8am–10pm

The Wydown Coffee Shop

Serious coffee experience (minus the skim milk).

1924 14th Street NW

W

thewydown.com

Mon–Fri 7am–3pm
Sat & Sun 8am–4pm

The Wydown is one of those places that goes about its business quietly—but very well. In a handy location to get some pre-shopping caffeine before browsing Miss Pixie's (see p.194), GoodWood (see p.199), and Outrage (see p.198), this place serves up pour-overs, espressos, and more to those in the know. It's pretty small, however, so its blond-wood tables are a commodity among the gym junkies, laptop aficionados, and younger folk who live in the area.

Nonetheless, I personally love that it has a strict no-skim-milk policy. If you don't want whole (or soy) milk, though, it's still worth a visit: All the coffees are delicious black, thanks to the quality beans.

Baked goods give a sugary pick-me-up, though there's no food beyond that. On H Street is a second, very beautiful location that morphs into a cocktail bar by night.

A Baked Joint

Cool, industrial-chic hangout with outdoor seating and great coffees.

---

430 K Street NW

W

abakedjoint.com

Mon & Tues 7:30am–2pm
Wed–Fri 7:30am–8:30pm
Sat & Sun 8am–8:30pm

A young professional crowd packs A Baked Joint, drawn by its excellent coffees, from flat whites to iced chai lattes, and a satisfying menu that leans heavily on the house-made bread and other baked goods.

All-day breakfasts and lunches include the biscuit sammie, an American-style biscuit (Australians and Brits, think: savory scone) with a fried egg and a choice of bacon, ham, or goat cheese, held together with a smear of mayo. My fave? The short-rib sammie, on griddle-toasted house-made sourdough. There are excellent veggie options too.

Brunch-goers pack the joint on weekends, making it hard to score a bench seat at the limited number of tables, but any other time is a more relaxed affair. In summer, it's a good spot to unwind over a 16-ounce cold brew.

The revamped neighborhood is just north of Chinatown and east of Mount Vernon Square. Given the new buildings and few trees, it's an unshaded walk from downtown, but there's a bikeshare station nearby.

La Colombe

Philadelphia coffee roaster brings great beans to a cool alley.

—————————————————

924 Blagden Alley NW

lacolombe.com

Mon–Fri 7am–6pm
Sat & Sun 8am–6pm

Fast expanding across the US, Philadelphia-based La Colombe gets my vote for one of DC's most consistent coffees in both roasting and brewing. Of the chain's five locations in the District, this one is by far my fave, in a lovely refurb of an old brick building, very tastefully done so it's all light and air.

It's hidden away, and finding it is half the fun: Look for redbrick footpaths leading into the center of the block bounded by N, M, 9th, and 10th Streets. Choose from the impressive rotating selection of varieties, and lounge about if there's space (the line can run out the door on weekends, but the rest of the time you'll probably get a seat at the narrow strip of tables). Back outside, the alley's murals present plenty of photo ops for colorful selfies—you may recognize the rainbow LOVE mural from Instagram.

Café Unido

Panamanian coffee of the highest quality in a Latino lifestyle market.

1280 4th Street NE

W

lacosechadc.com/
merchants/cafe-unido

Mon–Wed 8am–3pm
Thurs–Sun 8am–6pm

Housed in La Cosecha (see p.201), a collection of Latin American–themed shops in the Union Market District, Café Unido is an outpost of a Panamanian coffee chain. The founders source the beans directly from growers in Panama and support community projects in the country.

Before or after browsing the neighboring shops, settle in at one of the counter stools and enjoy anything from a pour-over to a nitro cold espresso. Tea lovers are met halfway with cascara, the steeped dried fruit surrounding the coffee bean; it makes a tangy, mildly caffeinated hot drink that tastes nothing like coffee. But top billing goes to Unido's complex Panamanian Geisha, one of the world's most expensive coffee varieties.

The Village DC

*Community-minded café that's bigger
than the coffee.*

Kevon King, Lauren Coles, and Mahammad Mangum opened this wonderful café in 2018 in part as a showcase for the talents of creative folks of color, to support budding entrepreneurs with workshop space and help them build their communities. Ideally head here on a weekend, when market stalls set up within the café space, and you'll find local makers selling everything from beauty products to high-quality handicrafts.

Admirably, the café side of the business—that is, the "excuse" most people have for visiting—is *very* good, especially the coffee. You might catch a whiff of fresh beans, roasted by a local company, Lone Oak, from a block away. The café's skilled baristas, who preside behind a modern blond-wood coffee bar, whip up everything from macchiatos to vanilla lattes. Regulars love the selection of seasonal flavored drinks, such as lavender-honey coffees.

As for food, it's a healthy and refreshingly unique selection of light bites, all made from local ingredients. One sublime example? The A.M. Sandwich: a brioche bun with bacon and egg, plus rich truffle-laced gouda.

The café is also located next to a branch of the wonderful bookstore Politics and Prose (see p.202), in case you're in the mood for a high-brow read to go with your brew.

1272 5th Street NE	thevillagedc.space	Tues–Fri 8am–3pm
		Sat & Sun 9am–4pm

Yellow

Casual café spiced with
Middle Eastern baked delights.

This order-at-the-counter café is a bright spark along Wisconsin Avenue in Georgetown. It's part of a restaurant group run by chef Michael Rafidi, the brains and skills behind celebrated Michelin-starred Albi, in Navy Yard. Rafidi has Jordanian-Palestinian roots, and Yellow's offerings—baked pastries, wood-fire-kissed pita sandwiches, and mezze—hum with Levantine and North African flavors. The za'atar croissant, a flaky French-style pastry oozing whipped labneh, always gets my taste buds singing. The ras el hanout morning bun, warm with a Moroccan spice mix, is tasty too, though offerings change seasonally so expect other sugary treats. More substantial bites include the pita sandwich stuffed with smoked lamb shoulder.

Yellow has lured some good baristas, and the beans are DC's own Counter Culture, though drink prices are on the high side. Plonk yourself down in one of two sunny seating areas, one with regular tables, the other with cushioned benches and casual lounge chairs.

After summer 2023, look out for a second Yellow in Union Market District, an extra-large version with an adjoining restaurant and "habibi funk" bar.

📍	w	🕑
1524 Wisconsin Avenue	yellowthecafe.com	Tue–Sun 8am–3pm

COCKTAIL CULTURE

DC is a "spirited" city—a tradition with roots as deep as George Washington distilling whiskey at Mount Vernon and John Adams swilling hard cider for breakfast. The gin rickey, a refreshing highball with lime and soda, was allegedly invented here in the late 1800s, and during Prohibition, bootleggers kept city residents well watered. On the law's repeal in 1934, DC native son Duke Ellington commemorated free drinking with the hit "Cocktails for Two."

DC's drinking culture hasn't slowed down since, with a profusion of saloons, neo-speakeasies, hotel rooftops, craft breweries, and more. Mixologists take their craft very seriously, often using spirits distilled in Virginia and Maryland to ensure a local flavor. Cocktail prices start around $12, but the more upmarket spots can hit you for around $25, especially if there's a view involved. Happy hour—in fact two or three hours, usually early evening weekdays—is the perfect opportunity to try new spots on the cheap; check websites for details.

Dirty Habit

Sleek and sophisticated bar-restaurant with a split personality.

---

555 8th Street NW

dirtyhabitdc.com

Mon–Thurs 7–10:30am,
11am–2pm & 5–10pm
Fri 7–10:30am,
11am–2pm & 5–11pm
Sat 9am–2pm & 5–11pm
Sun 9am–3pm & 5–9pm

Dirty Habit is an anomaly. Located within a basketball toss of the Capital One Arena, this lounge somehow manages to satisfy both the sports fans who roll through here on game nights and a see-and-be-seen clientele who head here for a glamorous night out.

Wedged between charming historic buildings, this sprawling place has three distinct areas: a dining room with a cocktail bar (propped up by two giant marble feet), an adjoining smart bar-restaurant area known as the Glass House, and an outdoor patio. All three serve classic cocktails and contemporary riffs, plus a fantastic range of nonalcoholic options. For lounging in style, the outdoor Patio Bar has comfortable long couches, hanging globes, and sleek firepits, and is typically filled with well-heeled young thangs.

Indoors, the Glass House is also a globally inspired restaurant at the top of its game; the 48-hour-braised short rib is a winner. Slightly cheaper offerings come during happy hour, Monday to Friday 3pm to 7pm.

Off the Record

Great drinks and political gossip in a place where the walls do talk.

800 16th Street NW

W

hayadams.com

Sun–Thurs 11:30am–12am
Fri & Sat 11:30am–12:30am

This bar bills itself as "Washington's place to be seen and not heard," but given that it's a step from the White House, these walls may have sprung a few leaks, as journalists used to rub shoulders here with politicos. These days, OTR buzzes with Capitol staffers who head here to unwind in elegance: plush red seating, pressed-tin ceilings, and old-fashioned service.

Despite the sophisticated aura, it doesn't take itself too seriously. The caricatures of politicians on the walls and coasters will have you in stitches. My favorite area is the Bench, a cozy nook framed by pictures of the Supreme Court judges.

Old-school cocktails make an appearance, but so too do the likes of A Senator's Secret and My Facts Are Facts Too. Given it's part of the beautiful Hay-Adams Hotel, prices are elevated (cocktails around $24), and yes, you'll want to dress the part.

Vue

Surprisingly accessible rooftop hotel bar with landmark vistas.

515 15th Street NW

W

thehotelwashington.com

Mon–Thurs 5pm–12am
Fri 5pm–2am
Sat 11am–2am
Sun 11am–12am

Even on the most humid of DC days, this place is pleasant. Located on the Hotel Washington's 11th floor (almost a skyscraper, by DC standards!), the appropriately named Vue doles out double charms: iconic landmarks such as the White House and the Washington Monument, as well as a changing menu of seasonal cocktails.

The terrace is split into two bars, each with a different vista. On weekends it expands to the Sky Room, a contemporary indoor-outdoor area. This place definitely gives you the "wow, I'm really in DC" feeling, albeit at a cost (cocktails start at $22). That said, it's not the priciest hotel bar, the atmosphere is not as fancy as you might expect, and, surprisingly, you don't need to reserve if you're coming in for a drink (though the restaurant does require booking). Overall, it's pleasantly casual and pulls in everyone from local workers to hotel guests and passing tourists.

Top of the Gate

Delivers scandal, architecture, and sublime sunsets.

2650 Virginia Avenue NW

thewatergatehotel.com

March–Oct
Thurs & Fri 4:30–11pm
Sat 4:30pm–12am

I'm partial to a scandal, and this bar comes with one, thanks to its location on the roof of the Watergate Hotel. The name is of course synonymous with career-ending political scandal, thanks to the 1972 break-in, ordered by President Nixon himself, to the Democratic party offices that were located in the building adjoining the hotel.

These days, though, the only real shocker is the hefty price tag ($25! Call it Cocktail-gate?) for seasonal concoctions such as the rum-and-ginger Rock Creek. But you're also paying for stunning 360-degree views of DC. Stroll around the open deck and admire the Potomac River, the Washington Monument, the Georgetown waterfront, and even the quirky sail shaped curves of the whole Watergate complex.

The vibe is one of expensive perfume: a sophisticated crowd imbibing high-quality drinks over a beautiful sunset, gourmet pizzas, and dishes of tapas.

The bar is open from spring through fall, weather permitting; reservations are recommended. In winter, head to the Next Whisky Bar, in the hotel lobby.

The Rooftop at the Graham

Rooftop gem with a pretty terrace and local vistas.

Set atop a boutique hotel, this is one of Georgetown's more sophisticated drinking haunts; you have to be over 21, and there's a business-casual dress code. Still, even though it's striving for a "see and be seen" scene, the result is not too snooty. The ambience on the small roof deck (it's covered and heated in winter) is intimate, with the feel of a private party. Usually you'll find businessy hotel guests and groups preparing for (or coming from) a night out.

The mixologists strut their stuff by shaking up the classics (Negronis, Manhattans) as well as their creations (an Is Good is a good mix of basil, vodka, and lime). Bar snacks like arancini and flatbreads aren't bad, but the drinks are better.

Come around sunset, grab a seat on one of the comfy couches, and admire the view of Georgetown on one side and, off in the distance on the other side, the Kennedy Center and the Monument.

1075 Thomas Jefferson
Street NW

thegrahamgeorgetown.com

Sun–Wed 4–10pm,
Thurs–Sat 4pm–12am

The Tombs

Raucous drinking den for students,
alumni, and others…

A subterranean haunt under a Federal-style town house, this place, with its walls bedecked in sports regalia and overall clubby feel, evokes an archetypal American student drinking den as seen on screens big and small (indeed, it was a setting for the 1980s film *St. Elmo's Fire*).

Students—many from nearby Georgetown University—gather nightly to knock back pints or pitchers of beer, and munch on affordable snacks such as chicken wings and cheesecake. Larger meals include the likes of eggplant parmigiana and beef stew. But let's face it, most are here for the grog.

Each day there's a deal of some sort, from half-price booze to a cheap "shot of the night." Happy hour is from 10pm onwards. Head here to make some friends, and expect a big night out (sometimes the party runs past posted closing time). On Sundays, churchgoing locals come here for brunch.

1226 36th Street NW

tombs.com

Mon & Tues 11am–1am
Wed & Thurs 11am–2am
Fri 11am–3am
Sat 11am–3am
Sun 10am–1am

The Green Zone

*Full-flavored Middle
Eastern bar with a
reggae beat.*

2226 18th Street NW

thegreenzonedc.com

Tues–Thurs 5pm–2am
Fri 5pm–3am
Sat 12pm–3am
Sun 12pm–2am

The Green Zone's Iraqi owner ran a pop-up bar for years, but fans finally convinced him to open a permanent space in 2018. Named for the International Zone in Baghdad, the bar is a cool mosaic-covered space with an explicitly welcoming mission: The events calendar includes Egyptian drag queens and Palestinian Ramadan dinners. The music may often be Latin reggae, but when it comes to food and drinks, the rhythm is Middle Eastern, as cocktails often incorporate ingredients from the region, such as arak, saffron, or fresh dates. And the food menu includes traditional meze, such as a falafel sandwich and muhammara (a red-pepper dip), as well as American bar snacks with a Middle Eastern twist, like chicken wings spiced with za'atar and sumac.

There's seating outside—particularly appealing in summer, when a boozy mint-lemonade is firmly on the menu—and a cozy upstairs open Thursday to Saturday. Happy hour is 5pm to 8pm Tuesday to Friday, as well as noon to 8pm Saturdays, and it serves a solid weekend brunch from noon to 3:30pm.

Jack Rose Dining Saloon

Whisk(e)y lovers, get ready to sip and taste.

2007 18th Street NW

W

jackrosediningsaloon.com

Wed 5pm–12am
Thurs & Fri 5pm–1am
Sat 4pm–2am
Sun 4–10pm

This smart watering hole boasts a selection of more than 2,500 bottles of both whisky and whiskey; some date back as far as 1915. It naturally draws a crowd that knows their Glenlivet from their Maker's Mark, though it also offers a range of cocktails, American craft beers, and international wines.

The atmosphere has a conservatives-in-cuff-links vibe, smart and tunnel-like with dark wood and a marble-top bar. And the walls are covered in all those bottles, from floor to ceiling. Side banquettes provide intimate spaces, while a roof terrace is lovely in summer.

Decent bar snacks such as Maryland-crab deviled eggs and whiskey wings satisfy pangs. Main meals trend toward modern American and meaty (price-wise too), with the likes of lamb porterhouse and burgers. Happy hour, which knocks $2 off drinks and bar snacks, is Wednesday to Friday 5pm to 7:30pm.

Lucky Buns

*Friendly place for chill cocktails and
mighty good burgers.*

You'll know you're in the right place when you spot the Eiffel Tower replica above the door—which is there not because this joint is French, but because it's too focused on its burgers and drinks to bother redecorating from the previous business. You're in a win-win situation: To start with, Lucky Buns serves what's frequently lauded as one of the country's best burgers. I confess that I came here with some skepticism, given the hype, but I was quickly converted; it's now a fave. According to owner, Chef Alex McCoy, "these are not Americana smash burgers, but a bolder 'take' with stronger flavors, thanks to locally sourced sustainable meats topped with in-house pickles and sauces."

But this place is listed alongside other bars because the drinks are solid too: Friendly mixologists shake together some of the city's most fun and colorful drinks with a tropical theme. Many of the macerations, including the root beer, are made in house. There's a shaded outdoor patio and a relaxed indoor area with hanging shades and wooden tables.

2000 18th Street NW

luckybuns.com

Mon–Thurs 5pm–12am
Fri 5pm–1am
Sat 11am–3pm &
5pm–1am
Sun 11am–3pm &
5pm–12am

Chicken + Whiskey

Coop yourself up in a chicken-centric diner followed by a speakeasy.

1738 14th Street NW

W

chickenandwhiskey.com/
14thstreet

Mon & Tues 5–10pm
Wed & Thurs 5pm–12am
Fri 5pm–2am
Sat 3pm–2am
Sun 3–10pm

If the two-in-one name has you scratching your head, it becomes a bit clearer when you enter. First, there's a nondescript fast-casual restaurant (open from 11am), with bright-yellow stools and a menu of Peruvian roast chicken (by the quarter, half, or whole bird) scrawled in vivid hues on a wall.

In the rear, a freezer door acts as a slightly contrived speakeasy entrance to an unexpectedly smart whiskey den lit with Edison bulbs. The bar's recycled-wood shelves are lined with 99 whiskeys, from Japan, Ireland, and beyond. An indicator of the largely young professional crowd: One cocktail is named Bitcoin Betty.

Monday's happy hour runs all day (the rest of the week is 5pm to 7pm), with all whiskeys discounted 25 percent. As for the chicken, don't walk past it: Brined and slow rotisserie-roasted in a wood-charcoal oven, it's good and good value.

Jane Jane

Retro cocktail bar with smart '50s-throwback vibes.

1705 14th Street NW

janejanedc.com

Mon–Wed 5pm–12am
Thurs 5pm–1am
Fri 5pm–2am
Sat 2pm–2am
Sun 2pm–12am

You can't help but smile at the décor of this cozy cocktail bar, with its mélange of full-on fun and breezy style: plaid-pattern mosaic tiles, teak-colored trim, and vintage-look wallpaper that could make you scream, "Classic cocktail, please!" (Indeed, the volume can be quite high here, partly because of the youngish crowd, and partly due to the lack of soundproofing.)

Classics such as martinis and Last Words feature strongly on the menu, but so too do 12 or so creative house riffs on staples. Gin lovers, don't go past the Gin-Soaked Felon, a concoction with elderflower, grapefruit, and Americano. Then, sit back, cradle your midcentury-style glass, and enjoy a retro snack (pigs in a blanket, anyone?).

Service is attentive and welcoming. The place doesn't take reservations, so it's a good idea to nab a seat early for happy hour (Monday to Thursday, 5pm to 7pm), when wines and beers are $6 and cocktails are $10.

Left Door

*Unexpectedly polished cocktail bar hidden behind
an unmarked door.*

While the contemporary faux speakeasy has manifested in all sorts of gimmicky entrances, from freezers to false bookshelves, this place feels more historically accurate, just for its lack of pretension: At the corner of 14th Street is a slightly grubby, simply marked door. There's a keypad, but no passcode is needed—push the door and head upstairs to an intimate, brick-lined space, a former apartment that's still furnished like one. The 1930s armchairs, wooden tables, and vintage dressers beam you into the elegant home of a great-great-aunt.

Behind the marble bar, enthusiastic mixologists shake to their lemon-zested heart's content. A limited but inventive list of changing specials have rarer ingredients, such as Japanese whiskeys. Drinks cost around $18 and are served in pretty glassware.

The space seats only 28, and no one is allowed to stand, so call to make a reservation and plan to stay a while: The drinks are worth lingering over.

1345 S Street NW

W

instagram.com/leftdoordc

Sun–Thurs 5pm–2am
Fri & Sat 5pm–3am

Lucy Bar

Corner bar with a Floridian vibe, handy for aperitifs.

1350 Florida Avenue NW

lucybardc.com

Mon–Thurs 5pm–12am
Fri 5pm–2am
Sat 1pm–2am
Sun 1pm–12am

This is a cheery spot for a predinner drink should you be dining on 14th Street (it's next to Maydan; see p.133). Perhaps inspired by its Florida Avenue address, it goes for a sunnier vibe, with bright aqua tiles and massive windows, a welcome change from windowless speakeasies. In fact, the very staged, super-bright décor invites Instagrammers (love the retro globe!). But that's half its fun.

The cocktails are varied—not all tropical—and a standard wine list is available too. The Patio Pounders section is ideal in summer, with a generous Aperol spritz and two frozen boozy drinks.

If you've got the munchies, decent pizzas fill the gap, though I'm a fan of the lasagna (and yes, the chef is Italian). It gets noisy, though in the summer, outdoor tables offer an escape. Happy hour runs Monday to Friday 5pm to 7pm.

All Souls

Cool, low-key neighborhood drinking den.

725 T Street NW

allsoulsbar.com

Mon–Thurs & Sun 5pm–2am
Fri & Sat 5pm–3am

An American answer to a British local or an Aussie pub, this is just a regular off-the-beaten-path corner bar in Shaw. I include it here, well, because it's just nice to have one place with no particular scene or Insta-op, where you can turn up anytime and easily order a beer or a cocktail (order by number from the "cocktail library": No. 2 is the Perfect Manhattan; No. 7 is a French 75). Then you can prop up the curved bar and chat with other regulars, or find a seat outside on the delightful patio, sheltered from the street by a low wall of plants.

The chill vibe here might entice you to stay all evening, just as other clients, from first-daters to those heading home from work, end up doing. The place doesn't serve food, but you can bring in your own; there's a pizza spot nearby.

El Techo

Cheap(ish) and cheerful Mexican-themed rooftop bar.

---

606 Florida Avenue NW

W

eltechodc.com

Mon–Thurs 5pm–12am
Fri 5pm–1:30am
Sat 12pm–1:30am
Sun 12pm–11pm

Tacos and burritos, creative cocktails, and a good-value happy hour will have you singing from *el techo* (the roof). This Mexican place is spread across a massive deck decorated with lanterns, palms, and bright murals.

A youngish, fun-loving crowd digs in to gut-busting tacos and signature toasted burritos. Don't go past the birria taco, which is filled with eight-hour braised lamb; there's a couple of veggie options too.

Margaritas are the standouts of the liquor list, and there are four to choose from. The spicy mezcal margarita delivers a kick, while the passion fruit variety is a tart favorite, especially when the heat hits. If you're with a crowd, get a pitcher (S40) or a skull (yes, you read that correctly) for S80. Tuesdays bring the best deal: three tacos and your choice of beer or margarita for S20.

Licht Café

Step into the light at this LGBTQIA+ living-room lounge.

1520 U Street NW

lichtdc.com

Mon–Thurs 4–11pm
Fri 4pm–1am
Sat 11am–1am
Sun 11am–11pm

Licht is the German word for light, and that's exactly what you get here in this inviting, sun-filled café-bar that caters to the District's queer community—not that you'd know from the outside, in a line of grungy row houses. But climb the stairs and step inside for a definite "wow" moment. Cheeky (in every sense) art lines the walls, and funky lighting adds to the glam.

The owner, Spencer, has a good eye for design and has conjured up a very sleek living room with a modern leather sofa, stylish green chairs, midcentury-modern chandeliers, and Moroccan-style rugs.

The tiny bar serves up big things: classic cocktails that cost a ridiculously good $12. This is a great place to meet people, queer or otherwise, and all are definitely welcome.

Lost & Found

Convenient neighborhood drinking den stuffed with locals and fun "junk."

1240 9th Street NW

W

lostandfounddc.com

Mon–Thurs 4pm–2am
Fri 4pm–3am
Sat 2pm–3am
Sun 2pm–2am

This place has two adjoining bar areas, one with a door on 9th Street and another with an entrance from Blagden Alley. Either way, it's my pick for a warm neighborhood feel. Plus I enjoy perusing its decorations: interesting castoffs amassed by one of the owners, an avid collector who finally found a wall or three on which to display his vinyl records and license plates. Even some of the seats are from the now disused RFK Stadium, while the Blagden Alley–side bar is made from a former bowling lane.

The long list of American craft beers and whiskeys is impressive yet affordable. Old-fashioneds and Manhattans are the top cocktail choices, but the professional bartenders shake up some unique numbers too. Note there's no food except for packaged snacks, your classic soaker-uppers only: potato chips and beef jerky, so unless it's a "liquid diet" kind of evening, this is the type of place you pop into before or after a meal.

Lulu's

Enjoyable and welcoming plant-filled wine garden.

1940 11th Street NW

luluswinegarden.com

Tues–Thurs 5–11pm
Fri 4pm–12am
Sat 12pm–12am
Sun 12pm–10pm

The place bills itself as a "casual-yet-chic, backyard wine bar." The chic part might be a tad overstated, but it's pleasant all the same. Filled with long communal tables and lively conversation, it's also a welcoming locale for solo travelers, who can sit at the bar; the bartenders are very approachable. And unlike many wine-centric spots, it's refreshingly unpretentious, attracting a diverse crowd of thirtysomethings to its sprawling space: part lounge, part veranda, part garden, with several patios and real plants. Plus the outdoor areas are covered and heated in winter.

    You can enjoy wines by the glass, though bottles dominate the list, which ranges across the US, Mexico, Argentina, and Europe.

Morris American Bar

*Pretty, classy cocktail bar with a
(non)-Prohibition purpose.*

It's no coincidence that this gorgeous bar—all pale blue and gray, with quirky
picture frames and comfortable seating—oozes *discreet* elegance: Its vision
is all about the Prohibition era, when drinkers were forced by law into secret
boozing. The name is a nod to Morris Sheppard, the senator responsible
for the short-lived 18th Amendment, which banned alcohol in the United
States—but also inspired a creative decade of cocktail invention. In honor, two
caricatures of Morris and his wife hang on the wall.

Naturally, classic cocktails are available, but the ever-changing menu
highlights quirky tropical numbers and even (1920s bootleg tipplers would be
shocked!) spirit-free cocktails.

Taco Tuesdays double as Tinder Tuesdays, when youngish hopefuls
come for $10 cocktails and a romantic vibe; happy hour is 5pm to 7pm on
Wednesdays and Thursdays.

1020 7th Street NW

morrisbardc.com

Tues–Thurs 5pm–1am
Fri & Sat 5pm–2am
Sun 5pm–12am

Right Proper Brewing Company

The place to go for house-brewed "crafties".

The outdoor tables and umbrellas near the Howard Theatre Walk indicate you've arrived at Right Proper. The craft brewer's interior is surprisingly funky-arty, with a couple of long bars, designer lighting, and exposed brick, painted with whimsical murals, all by local artists. You can view the workings of the five-barrel brewing system through the glass behind the bar.

The house brew selection rotates to cater to the regulars, beer drinkers of the trimmed-beard variety. Nonetheless, the two flagship brews—Raised by Wolves (a dry-hopped pale ale) and Senate Beer (an American-style light lager)—are usually on offer.

The creative gastropub-style cuisine matches the surrounds. "Sharesies" include beer-batter cheese curds or cauliflower, and the kitchen nails the entrees: an excellent burger, satisfying steak frites, and a generous tofu bowl. All very right and proper!

	W	⌄
624 T Street NW	rightproperbrewing.com	Mon–Thurs 12pm–10pm
		Fri & Sat 12pm–11pm
		Sun 12pm–9pm

Service Bar

Good, solid, reliable drinking den.

---

926 U Street NW

servicebardc.com

Tues–Thurs 5pm–2am
Fri 5pm–3am
Sat 2pm–3am
Sun 4pm–2am

When it first opened, Service Bar was billed as the place where service-industry folk go after their late shifts end. These days, almost everyone seems to head here for its buzz and a laid-back vibe. As the night progresses, the music gets turned up (local bands play here too); it can be loud and rowdy but is fun, fun, fun.

The friendly mixologists are happy to experiment with unusual combos, along with offering the classics and fresh tropical drinks. With drinks going for around $14, it's one of the best-value bars around.

The kitchen, meanwhile, serves solid, elevated pub food, and its fried chicken gets the thumbs-up from hungry patrons. I like the chicken too, especially with a Mango Sticky Rice. That's a cocktail, by the way: a foam-topped blend of rhum agricole, shochu, mango, coconut, and more.

Copycat Co.

Opium-den feel with cool cocktails and Chinese snacks.

1110 H Street NE

copycatcompany.com

Wed, Thurs & Sun 5pm–2am
Fri & Sat 5pm–3am

You'll hardly be the first to discover this funky, dimly lit slip of a bar, but being a "copycat" is a compliment here: You're following in good footsteps, particularly restaurant workers in their after-shift wind-down hours.

The draw, first of all, is the shared plates of authentic Chinese street food, such as dumplings and bao buns; I'm a sucker for the mapo tofu. The strong cocktails are another attraction. They change seasonally, but you might find something like a Quirky Flip (strawberry, coconut, port, sherry, and rye) or an Apples and Oranges (citrus, allspice, falernum, bitters, and applejack). Stick with the classics or customize your own concoctions. My friend Sarah, who insists on requesting such orders as "gin and melancholy" or "tequila and happiness," swears these bartenders are up to the challenge.

Cotton & Reed

Laid-back boutique distillery with cocktails all built around rum.

1330 5th Street NE

W

cottonandreed.com

Mon–Thurs 4pm–12am
Fri 4pm–2am
Sat 12pm–2am
Sun 12pm–10pm

Don't expect beer. Don't order wine. "We are a rum distillery. Just FYI," the menu clarifies. It's also, however, a compact, friendly bar that's handily located bang in the heart of Union Market District. Industrial-style stools and one long wooden bar with a metal frame make it feel a bit like a school science lab.

That's appropriate given that the two owners (Reed Walker and Jordan Cotton) were NASA personnel before they got into distilling. The real chemistry happens out back (tours of the distillery run on Saturdays and include a cocktail, for $20). In the front tasting room, compare rums with a flight, be a purist with a daiquiri, or try one of the strong cocktails that take rum in new directions—such as the Rumba Palumba ("rum and mezcal are friends," advises the menu) and a surprising fermented take on a piña colada.

To soak up the proof, you're allowed to bring in your own food (there's reasonable takeout right nearby). No reservations, so just rock on up.

Last Call

1301-A 4th Street NE

W

lastcallbardc.com

Mon–Fri 5pm–late

Sat & Sun 12pm–late

True to its name, this drinking den is open until...well, whenever they decide to close (though it's usually around 2am or 3am). And yes, it's a dive bar, though not in a this-floor's-been-getting-stickier-for-thirty-years way, but more in a no-frills, wear-whatever way. In fact, when the owner, Gina Chersevani, opened it in 2018 in a disused cafeteria, she might have started a new design trend: cocktail dive. Think peeling green and blue paint on the brickwork, a concrete floor, and industrial lights.

The well-priced drinks are sophisticated, despite names like Sip It, Don't Drip It (gin, lime, grapefruit, tonic) and a Filthy Martini. A short draft list with some DC-based brews attracts beer drinkers—and (here's where the dive bar vibe really comes in) $3 Jell-O shots get the party going. The ciabatta sandwiches *may* help soak things up; regular patrons swear by the brisket one, with caramelized onion and horseradish mayo, for a reasonable $10. Happy hour (daily 5pm to 7pm) yields even better deals.

The Betsy

*Ultra-casual neighborhood gin bar
hidden in a back alley.*

From Belga Café on 8th Street, follow the chicken footprints on the pavement through an alley and up the stairs to Betsy, a refreshingly indie, slightly grungy bar on a covered rooftop. There's no view, but you don't need one, as the decorations keep you stimulated: wall hangings, plants, kitsch souvenirs, and plastic flowers. In cool weather, blankets are on hand to keep you cozy.

It's a fun, casual spot that makes a good start (or end) to your night over a range of gins or a simple ale. Gin varieties range from Tanqueray to Himalayan productions, mixed up in a regular gin and tonic or a number of pretty luxe variations on the drink, cryptically categorized on the menu under Love, Sympathy, Passion, and Flirt.

You could also head here for dinner or weekend brunch. Shared plates and bites—such as crispy brussels sprouts, brie-topped waffles, and pots of mussels—are from Belga Café below. Happy hour is 4:30pm to 5:30pm Tuesday to Friday. Oh, and if you're wondering, Betsy is the owner's hen, the pick of the coop.

Q	**W**	**◡**
514 8th Street SE	thebetsyusa.com	Mon–Sun 4:30pm–late
		(weather permitting)

Bluejacket

Massive, vat-filled craft brewery and beer hall.

Set in historic Navy Yard, this impressive manufacturing building harks back to 1919, when it was a boilermaker shop within the larger shipyard. These days, its industry is beer, as you'll see from the giant silver vats that are visible through the large windows. The renovated space combines both brewing and seating for 200 people across various levels.

Beer director Greg Engert takes all things hops very seriously and turns out a good range of traditional porters, classic lagers, and bold IPAs. The selection rotates regularly, but you can expect about 20 Bluejacket beers and five cask ales on tap.

Soak it up with some classic yet refined beer-hall fare: burgers and meaty sandwiches, as well as salads and grilled fish (the kitchen closes at 10:30pm).

The atmosphere is buzzy—it's a fun place to meet a group—but note the noise factor, thanks to the wide-open plan and lots of steel.

	W	
300 Tingey Street SE	bluejacketdc.com	Mon–Thurs 11am–12am
		Fri & Sat 11am–1:30am
		Sun 11am–9:30pm

EPIC EATS

Once largely limited to greasy-spoon diners and white-tablecloth steakhouses, DC eateries didn't show much variation or character. The only bright spot was in immigrant-run kitchens, but visitors rarely stumbled across them. But now, foodies, rejoice! Over the past decade, the District's chefs have sharpened their knives and carved out a local cuisine scene. The revival of many of the central neighborhoods has encouraged homegrown chefs and supported new personalities. Historically, DC has favored a blend of Southern-style soul food and assorted seafood, and these remain firmly on menus. In addition, now seasonal local produce, sourced from Maryland, Virginia, and Pennsylvania, finds its way into creative dishes for adventurous palates. And the locals are gobbling it up.

You'll find everything from coffee spots to Michelin-starred restaurants. Reservations are encouraged in the evenings, as not even turning up at the start of service can always guarantee a seat: Locals tend to eat early. Nonetheless, you can often get a seat at the bar.

Mitsitam Native Foods Café

The Mall's best eating option is at the National Museum of the American Indian.

4th Street &
Independence Avenue SW

W

mitsitamcafe.com

Mon–Sun 11am–5pm

USD

$$

Museum cafeterias in DC can range from poor to poorer, in my opinion. But Mitsitam is a welcome improvement—and really the only decent place to eat on the Mall aside from the food trucks that line 14th Street and 7th Street.

Mitsitam serves a changing menu of Native foods from across the Americas. This can include dishes like Bolivian-style chile-braised pork shanks and wild salmon cooked on a cedar plank, as well as tacos with prickly pear mole and a pulled-buffalo sandwich. Grab a seat at the windows, which curve around with the building, and overlook the Mall.

Bindaas

*Fabulous high-end
Indian street food at
low-end prices.*

2000 Pennsylvania
Avenue NW

W
bindaasdc.com

Mon–Sun 11:30am–9pm

USD
$$

Upmarket Indian snacks are the mission
of this cheerful corner spot. Bright-orange
umbrellas and potted plants on the sidewalk
indicate you've found the right place, while
fun frescoes and photographs of Indian
scenes cover the restaurant's interior.

Bindaas is in the stable of Ashok
Bajaj, who made his name with the excellent
Rasika (see p.110), and it has similarly high
quality, though with a more casual approach.
Dishes hail from all over India, with samosas,
chaat (savory snacks), buns, and kebabs,
plus a few more substantial dishes like
chicken tikka masala and vegetable korma.
The dahi papdi chaat (with chickpeas and
pomegranate seeds) and pao bhaji (buns
with veggie stew) alone are worth the
pilgrimage here. The price-to-quality ratio
is among the best in DC. An even cheaper,
fast-casual spot is Bindaas Bowls and Rolls,
at 415 7th Street NW.

Carmine's

Traditional family-style Italian that's also DC's biggest restaurant.

---

425 7th Street NW

W

carminesnyc.com/locations/washington-dc

Tues–Thurs 11:30am–9pm
Fri & Sat 11:30am–10pm
Sun 11:30am–9pm

USD
$$

Yes, this is part of a chain (the mother ship is in New York City), and yes, it's enormous, with 600 seats across various dining areas. But it still has a "just like Mamma used to make" charm—if Mamma specialized in old-school, red-sauce-drenched Italian American food. Indeed, the smell of that garlic-laced red sauce hits you as soon as you enter, and, with the family-style portions, you'll get literal piles of pasta. I alternate between the ragu and the lasagna, but others vouch for the veal parmigiana and veal or shrimp scaloppine.

Depending on which room you're in and what party you happen to be seated next to, the place can be loud. And it's not the cheapest option around. But overall it's a welcome alternative to sleeker, more formal dining, or cramped and casual eateries. And with those feed-a-family portions, it's great for groups. Be sure to save room for the desserts: As the man said in *The Godfather*, take the cannoli.

Levain Bakery

*Cookie cravings satisfied
like nowhere else.*

3131 M Street NW

W

levainbakery.com

Mon–Sun 8am–8pm

Levain Bakery got its start in 1995 in New York City when the two women founders met during—ironically—triathlon training. Since then, the bakery has built its reputation almost entirely on its chocolate-chip walnut cookie, distinctively crispy outside yet still a bit gooey inside. DC's M Street is home to a Levain branch, so you too can be sated by this sweet, energizing snack. Chocolate is at the core of most recipes, but if that's not your thing, try the oatmeal-raisin option. Note: They. Are. Big. Six ounces, and a couple of inches high.

All are baked on-site daily, and any leftovers are donated to charity, a practice they've followed since they first started baking (and were less sure of quantities). They're a great gift too, if you want an excuse to buy more than one.

China Chilcano

Fabulous Peruvian cuisine, in all its fusion glory.

One of the best of the many restaurants run by DC's kitchen guru José Andrés, this eatery showcases the multicultural heritage of Peru through its intertwined traditions of comida criolla (influenced by Spain and Africa), Chinese-inflected chifa dishes, and Japanese-style nikkei cuisine. What that means in practice: nigiri served on a bed of causa (mashed Peruvian potatoes) rather than rice, Pacific wild shrimp with fermented black beans, or a pot of crispy fried rice with pork belly.

The large industrial-chic space is filled with red Edison(ish) light bulbs, fabulous murals, and Tolix chairs. But discrete seating areas keep it cozy.

Book ahead to secure a table, but if you haven't, the place is big enough that if you turn up early, you should be able to snare a spot.

418 7th Street NW

W

chinachilcano.com

Mon–Thurs 4–10pm

Fri 4–11pm

Sat 11:30am–11pm

Sun 11:30am–10pm

USD

$$ to $$$

The Hamilton

Eclectic, centrally located spot that fits the bill when you want food and music.

600 14th Street NW

W

thehamiltondc.com

Mon–Sun 11am–2am

USD

$$

I've never really been able to work out this sprawling place, other than I've sat in all the different wood-paneled rooms—under quirky art nouveau lighting, over cocktails, with a meal, or for a show—and I've enjoyed it every time.

The Hamilton somehow manages to cater to an eclectic crowd of locals and tourists with various dining rooms and banquettes, a sushi bar, several bars for drinking, and, in the basement, an entertainment venue where acts range from jazz to hard rock.

As for the food, it bills itself as "inventive American" using regional produce; it's solid and not more. (I prefer the fresh choices at the sushi bar.) Still, with so many food, booze, and music options, you're bound to find a space that suits for a fun night out.

Old Ebbitt Grill

*American favorites in
a classy landmark
with good ambience.*

---

675 15th Street NW

W

ebbitt.com

Mon–Fri 11am–1am

Sat & Sun 10am–1am

USD

$$ to $$$

So renowned is Old Ebbitt that it had to be included in this book, despite there being other reasonable spots in the area. It may be the oldest saloon in Washington—at least in spirit, as it has moved several times since it opened in 1856. But even the current location, a former Beaux-Arts theater, feels quite classic, as it's been settled in here since 1983, and due to its proximity to the treasury and the White House, it was a longtime hangout for legislators and statesmen (definitely men at the time). It's the kind of place that still hands out matchbooks instead of business cards.

These days, it attracts fewer VIPs and plenty more tourists, who come to soak up the scenery of frescoed ceilings, massive oil paintings, romantic lamps, and a long mahogany bar.

The meals are classic American; the best dish is the crab cake. But come for early or late happy hour (3pm to 5pm and 11pm to 1am), especially for oysters. Old Ebbitt takes the bivalves very seriously, even serving them with an Oyster Eater's Bill of Rights.

Rasika

High-end Indian cuisine in a modern chic environment.

1190 New Hampshire
Avenue NW

W
rasikarestaurant.com

Mon–Thurs 11:30am–
2:30pm & 5–10pm
Fri 11:30am–2:30pm &
5–10:30pm
Sat 5–10:30pm
Sun 11am–2:30pm &
5–9pm

USD
$$ to $$$

Rasika is one of DC's best fine-dining options. Its upscale Indian cuisine and extremely professional service makes it among my personal favorites for a special night out.

In fact there are two Rasikas, the Penn Quarter flagship and this one in the West End, which I prefer for its buzz and modern atmosphere. The exterior, part of an office building, looks a bit impersonal, but the chic interior is warm and inviting, and you can dine at your choice of banquettes, tables, or the bar.

Particularly popular items on menu include the palak chaat (delicately fried spinach leaves with yogurt and date chutney) and the honey-glazed black cod. I concur, and add the chicken tikka masala and the lamb biryani. Worth noting too is the solid list of vegetarian dishes.

Tatte

Handy café for light meals with Middle Eastern zing.

1200 New Hampshire
Avenue NW

W

tattebakery.com

Mon–Sat 7am–8pm
Sun 8am–7pm

USD

$

One of a chain of seven around metro DC, Boston-based Tatte opened in 2020, but it's one of those places that you'd think has been here forever, such is its loyal following.

That loyalty is due to its focus on details: Tatte takes coffee very seriously, with a separate bar devoted to it. The owner's Israeli roots are revealed in a glass case piled high with an array of cakes laden with zingy zataar and crunchy sesame. (It must be said, to my palate, the pastries tend toward dry, though all the better for dipping into your coffee.)

Tatte nails brunch and lunch, with dishes like an open-face sandwich of smoked salmon, avocado, and egg or a shakshuka with lamb meatballs (instead of the usual egg) and a delicious blend of peppers.

The space is gorgeous too: light and airy, with white mosaic floors and black trim. There's a plant-lined outdoor patio that looks onto the street.

Call Your Mother

Super-popular outlet for impressive,
creative bagels and snacks.

With seven DC locations, this popular deli mini-chain bills itself as "Jew-*ish*": It's definitely not kosher, but its menu of bagels and classic sandwiches (such as whitefish salad) are inspired by the delicatessen tradition and made with very high-quality ingredients. Georgetown's outlet is among the most charming, for its corner setting in an old house painted eye-catching pink.

The colors draw the Instagrammers, but it's worth weaving your way past them for a hearty bagel with equally hearty schmears or sandwich fixings. You could start the day with, say, a bacon, egg, and multiple cheeses, with a drizzle of spicy honey. Another good option: avocado, Fritos (yes, the corn chips), red onion, and jalapeños.

You might have to wait in line, but it's the perfect place to meet students who pass by on the way to nearby Georgetown University. And it's the nearest thing to hearty, homey food, without having to, er, call your mother.

📍
3428 O Street NW

🕐
Mon–Sun 7:30am–2pm

USD
$

W
callyourmotherdeli.com

Foxtrot

Modern convenience store meets café meets floating office.

1267 Wisconsin Avenue NW

W

foxtrotco.com

Mon–Sun 7am–10pm

USD

$

With three locations in DC, this Chicago-based chain caters to fast-paced urban living, whether that means hunching over a laptop, powered by coffee, grabbing a healthy farro veggie bowl or avocado toast for lunch, or just racing in for a mini bottle of Moët.

The corner spot is light and airy, with a handy bank of tables and chairs at the window, ready-made boxed meals to one side, a coffee bar, and shelves of high-end local produce. For travelers, it's a good destination for a fast and affordable—but nourishing—lunch. And if you come with your laptop, expect some noise; others have made it their office *so* much that long Zoom calls are common.

Martin's Tavern

*Old-style pub that's
popular for past presidents.*

1264 Wisconsin Avenue NW

W

martinstavern.com

Mon–Thurs 11am–1:30am
Fri 11am–2:30am
Sat & Sun 8am–2:30am

USD

$$

Open since 1933, Martin's Tavern is proud of its streak of serving every sitting US president from the 1940s (Harry S. Truman) to the 2000s (George W. Bush). Barack Obama may have broken that streak, but Martin's is still popular for its cozy English pub vibe and hearty comfort food. Dig in to a bison burger or fish-and-chips for lunch or dinner, or slide into a booth on weekends for a carb-loaded brunch of pancakes or eggs Benedict.

Sure, there are cooler DC eateries that serve more contemporary cuisine. But there are few such places with a menu for all diets and budgets, or the tradition of this DC institution, not to mention its romantic vibe: Another major point of pride is that JFK proposed to Jackie Bouvier here (and yes, you can reserve that booth for your own occasion).

Green Almond Pantry

*Gourmet Mediterranean fare perfect
for a picnic lunch.*

Don't be fooled by the fact that this small, casual Mediterranean lunch counter and market is relegated to the back corner of mini food hall Grace Street Collective. Though a tiny space, it's a feast for the eyes and taste buds, thanks to its Turkish American owner, Cagla Onal-Urel, who brightens the place with bunches of fresh flowers, a large wooden communal table, and shelves full of organic eggs, olive oils, and tinned fish.

    The Mediterranean menu is perfect for a picnic in Georgetown Waterfront Park, just one block south. To make yourself a feast, grab a slab of Onal-Urel's renowned focaccia, then whatever looks good on the daily specials chalked up on the blackboard. These could be, for instance, mercimek koftesi (red-lentil balls) or a fresh green fava-bean dip. Even heartier dishes feature seasonal produce: a tart of local asparagus, ramps, and leeks, say.

📍	🕑	**USD**
3210 Grace Street NW	Tues & Wed 11:30am–3pm	$
W	Thurs–Sat 11:30am–7pm	
greenalmondpantry.com	Sun (market only) 11am–2pm	

Stachowski's

Butcher shop and grocery that's great for take-out deli sandwiches.

1425 28th Street NW

W

stachowskimarket.com

Mon–Sat 10am–8pm
Sun 11am–6pm

USD

$$

One of Georgetown's favorite neighborhood haunts, Stachowski's has been quietly wooing locals with its charcuterie and other gourmet offerings since 2011, though the owners have been curing meats for over 60 years.

For visitors, it's the perfect place to pick up a sandwich, especially if you're headed to nearby Tudor Place or Dumbarton Oaks, which both have lovely gardens. Or if you're done with sightseeing, take your sandwich for a picnic on the Georgetown Canal or in Waterfront Park.

"Sandwich," though, hardly captures the product: These are humongous piles of deliciousness that just happen to come between two bits of bread. While not the cheapest around, they are definitely the best value this side of the Earl of Sandwich's change purse. The hot pastrami (done in the classic style: on pumpernickel with mustard) is a winner, but meat-eaters also love the 4 Meat Grinder, featuring house-made salami, coppa, mortadella, and soppressata, along with pickled hot peppers and other trimmings.

Chiko

Satisfying flavors at this mini-chain where Chi-na *meets* Ko-rea.

2029 P Street NW

W

mychiko.com

Mon–Sun 11am–9pm

USD

$$

When partners Danny Lee and Scott Drewno opened Chiko, its fresh food, inspired by Chinese and Korean flavors and techniques, was an immediate hit, and the success has continued: There are now four metro-DC locations.

Fan favorites include Orange-ish Chicken, a vastly elevated rendition of the too-sweet take-out staple, as well as some of the best brussels sprouts in the city, thanks to spicy-sweet gochujang mayo. I also like the soy-glazed brisket with furikake-buttered rice and the kimchi stew with pork belly.

The original Dupont Circle Chiko is a "don't judge a book by its cover" situation, with a slightly shabby exterior and a nondescript interior—but the colors and flavors of the Asian delights do the work.

If you prefer not to navigate a half-flight of stairs at the entrance, head for the branch on the east side of Capitol Hill (423 8th Street SE), which is at street level. And for more atmosphere and exemplary Korean food, head to Lee and Drewno's smarter Anju, nearby on 18th Street.

Emissary

Café with good coffee and healthy brunch and lunch plates.

2032 P Street NW

W

emissarydc.com

Mon–Fri 7am–8pm
Sat 7:30am–8pm
Sun 8am–6pm

USD

$–$$

This cheerful spot is one of my regular go-tos near Dupont Circle. Housed in the basement of a quirky Queen Anne–style building, the brick-walled space, with a refurbished terrazzo floor, has several seating nooks, and outdoor tables with umbrellas provide seats for the passing P Street action.

Brunch gastronauts will love the smashed avocado toast (five stars for freshness!) and the organic-greens-and-quinoa bowl. The bean roasts are exceptional, and generally, baristas serve up great brews. The full coffee menu covers macchiato to flat white. Tea drinkers swear by the matcha latte.

Happy hour (4pm to 7pm Monday to Saturday) sees $8 wines and $7 beers. But anytime cocktails are excellent value at $12. I especially like the Negroni d'Emissary, made with local Ivy City gin.

Teaism

Fresh and healthy from DC's original fast casual.

2009 R Street NW

W

teaism.com

Mon–Sun 11am–8pm

USD

$$

This women-owned establishment is a fabulous healthy eating option, a rare-in-DC place for fast, light meals that aren't fried. Opened in 1996, it was ahead of the fast-casual trend, but has the sort of food you don't want to rush. Lunch meals (order at the counter, then take a table) include a substantial salmon bento box, Thai-style chicken curry, and palak paneer (Indian-spiced spinach with cheese).

But as the name indicates, tea is the original raison d'être: The menu lists some 50 varieties from all over the world. And their salty oatmeal cookies—plain, or with chocolate or raisins—are a longtime local favorite.

This Dupont Circle location has pleasant, umbrella-shaded outdoor seating, or you can opt for the cozy indoor space, with wooden stools and tables. There's also a location in Penn Quarter.

Federalist Pig

*Smokin' in DC: some of the nation's best barbecue
styles all under one roof.*

Before Federalist Pig arrived in 2016, DC's barbecue scene was medium-rare. This place changed all that. The staff work nearly 24 hours a day, tending the low-and-slow wood-fired smoker to produce perfectly tender beef brisket, turkey breast, and sausages, as well as pork ribs, shoulder, and belly.

Cuts are sold by the half-pound, piled directly onto a butcher-paper-lined tray, along with pickles and a thick slice of Texas toast. If you want something a bit more dressed up, opt for one of the sandwiches, such as pork with coleslaw and a Carolina-style vinegar sauce. Vegetarians aren't left out: There's a Vietnamese-style sandwich with crispy "tofu burnt ends." Sides are both traditional (smoky beans, mac and cheese) and otherwise (crispy brussels sprouts).

Like all the nation's most notable barbecue joints, the decor is basic: just a shedlike store, with a few outdoor tables and a string of lights. Go for lunch or an early dinner, as there's often a line, and the place closes when the day's product runs out.

📍	🕐	**USD**
1654 Columbia Road NW	Wed–Sun 11:30am–9pm	$$
	(or until sold out)	
W		
federalistpig.com		

Julia's Empanadas

Parcels of Latin American deliciousness make a convenient snack.

2452 18th Street NW

W

juliasempanadas.com

Mon–Thurs 10am–9pm
Fri & Sat 10am–3am
Sun 10am–8pm

USD

$

Chilean American Julia has been legendary in DC ever since she opened her first store, in 1993, and introduced the city to these handy little pockets of dough baked with a huge range of fillings.

Latin Americans argue over preferred fillings and styles, but Julia seems to cover all bases. You can sink your teeth into a Jamaican-style curried beef empanada or a chicken-and-potato salteña, a treat of Argentina and Bolivia, complete with egg and olive. There's also a veg-friendly spinach option, and always something for vegans.

The Adams Morgan location is open until a wild-for-DC 3am on Friday and Saturday, so handy for a late-night snack—and there's another location in Dupont Circle, closer to major sights, for when you want a quick lunch on the go.

Zenebech

This family-run Ethiopian restaurant is a DC institution.

2420 18th Street NW

W

zenebechdc.com

Mon–Thurs 5–10pm
Fri–Sun 1–10pm

USD

$$

·

This beloved restaurant was open in Shaw for 18 years, but relocated to Adams Morgan in 2017—then promptly suffered a fire, alarming all its loyal patrons who'd followed to the new neighborhood. Fortunately it reopened in 2018, better than ever. Grab a seat in this casual, no-fuss place, and you'll see why it has inspired such devotion. Genuine Ethiopian dishes await, appealing equally to carnivores, vegetarians, and vegans; most are gluten-free as well.

As for choices? The menu includes all the Ethiopian classics, especially well prepared. Kitfo is a marinated ground beef dish (or anything minced, in fact), and Zenebech's version is tops. Stir-fried tibs can be had with cubes of beef, chicken, or even lamb. Slow-cooked wot (stew) shows up with chicken, beef, or chickpeas. I love that each visit pushes me to try a different dish or two, all eaten with injera, the flat and spongy Ethiopian bread—and Zenebech's is excellent, because it was the foundation of the business that grew into a full restaurant.

Busboys and Poets

Feast on politics, books, and wholesome American fare.

2021 14th Street NW

W

busboysandpoets.com

Mon–Sun 9am–9pm

USD

$$

I love this expansive, down-to-earth spot for its general vibe and buzz. "Food, Books, Film, Coffee, Stage, Internet, Bar" reads the sign at the entrance, and this welcoming community hub delivers it all, to a huge range of people, from grandparents with families to DC's young professionals. You too will surely find something to like here: a new political read from the activist bookstore, perhaps, or a drink at the bar, or a poetry reading in the cultural center.

As for the food, it hits the right notes with all-out American dishes, including beef chili bowls and shrimp and grits (both highly recommended). For vegans there are some excellent options, such as the vegan burger. Efficient service and fair prices seal the deal. A second DC location is at 450 K Street NW, in Shaw.

Compass Rose

Globe-trot with your tastebuds in a glamorous neighborhood locale.

1346 T Street NW

W

compassrosedc.com

Tues–Sat 5–11pm
Sun 11am–10pm
Bar until late

USD

$$

The owners of this multilevel row house call themselves "armchair tasters," and so the menu here takes you on a virtual trip around the globe. Generous share dishes include sweet potato chaat from India, Jamaican-style lamb curry, Chinese short-rib bao buns, and Japanese veggie tempura, though the headliner is the Georgian khachapuri (cheese bread). To accompany, you can choose a "liquid journey of the world" too.

The interior's exposed-brick walls feature plant hangers and street art galore and, depending on which nook or cranny you're in, there are touches of velvet or fairy lights.

While Compass Rose could be criticized for trying to please the world, it does a pretty good job at it. Noise levels can be on the high side at weekend brunches.

Jeni's

Famous ice cream shop worthy of presidential visits.

1925 14th Street NW

W

jenis.com

Mon–Wed 12–11pm
Thurs & Fri 12pm–12am
Sat & Sun 11am–12am

USD

$

When you hit a line on the corner of 14th Street and Wallach Place, you know you've arrived at Jeni's. The organic ice cream company is known for its chunky and creative flavors, such as Powdered Jelly Donut, Blackout Chocolate Cake, and even Everything Bagel. Its Sunshine flavor (lemon, tangerine, passion fruit) is a jarring gray—but the taste is splendid. Though founded in Columbus, Ohio, Jeni's is considered a DC icon because politicos have come to love it; even President Biden made a pit stop here en route to a meeting.

DC has four Jeni's outlets, and this one is handy for a sugar fix when hoofing around the 14th Street and U Street corridors.

Honestly, I prefer the pure flavors of Italian gelato, but my ice-cream-lickin' friends would never speak to me again if this didn't make the cut.

Le Diplomate

Fancy French brasserie that pulls in the crowds.

1601 14th Street NW

W

lediplomatedc.com

Mon–Thurs 12pm–3pm
& 5–11pm
Fri 12pm–12am
Sat 9:30am–12am
Sun 9:30am–11pm

USD
$$$

One of DC's most revered spots, this super-busy brasserie is Parisienne from its vintage mirrors to its colorful woven bistro chairs. The menu is the real deal, with Gallic classics like onion soup gratinée and bouillabaisse—though there is also a "burger Américain" on the lunch menu. Personally, my finger never seems to get past the boeuf bourguignon or the steak frites.

As for desserts? There'd be something wrong with me if I didn't recommend the milk chocolate pot de crème. And the profiteroles. Oh, and the vanilla bean crème brûlée.

Whether out-of-towners or DC power brokers, everyone jostles to get a spot here, so reserve ahead in the evening. Out front, under the red awning, is cute patio seating for soaking up the view and the buzz of 14th Street.

All Purpose Pizza

Artisanal New Jersey–style pizzas in hip DC surrounds.

1250 9th Street NW

W

allpurposedc.com

Mon–Thurs 5–10pm
Fri 5–11pm
Sat 11am–2:30pm
& 5pm–11pm
Sun 11am–2:30pm
& 5–9pm

USD
$$

The aroma of oregano welcomes you to this friendly spot, a pizzeria in a far-from-traditional converted warehouse with a mosaic floor and funky lighting.

One of the two delightful owners, Michael Friedman, grew up in New Jersey, so he knows a thing or two about his pies. The dough is fermented for three days, and the 12-inch (30cm) pizzas are cooked in good old Jersey-pizzeria-style deck ovens longer than a typical Naples product, resulting in a delightfully crispy-chewy crust.

Toppings are a wonderful mélange of traditional and gourmet. Devotees love the Buona, a standard pepperoni pie with the kick of Calabrian chili honey, plus fresh basil and grated grana padana. For a year's worth of calcium, go for the Sedgewick, a quattro formaggi with gourmet cheeses and truffle honey.

Weekend brunches are fun, with bottomless mimosas or Aperol spritzes. The same team is behind the Red Hen (see p.134).

Ben's Chili Bowl

Historic landmark and famous Black-owned eatery.

1213 U Street NW

W

benschilibowl.com

Mon–Thurs &
Sun 11am–9pm
Fri & Sat 11am–4am

USD

$

Ben Ali, owner of the eponymous Chili Bowl, was born in Trinidad to Indian parents, before opening the restaurant in 1958 with his American-born wife, Virginia. Their place is famous for feeding those who made civil-rights history, including participants in the 1963 March on Washington with Martin Luther King, and it even kept serving throughout the 1968 riots, following MLK's assassination. Today, their sons still run this landmark.

Along with the history comes hearty (possibly heart-stopping) American diner food. The big favorite is the half-smoke, an only-in-DC version of a hot dog, with slightly chunkier meat and, yes, a hint of smoke. It's topped with mustard and onions and, optionally, Ben's spicy homemade chili (whether the traditional beef-and-bean version, one with turkey, or even a vegan option, which you can get on a veggie dog). A selection of subs and burgers are on the menu too, along with banana pudding.

Hanumanh

Blend of Laotian and other Asian delights.

1604 7th Street NW

W

hanumanh.com

Fri–Sun 5–10pm

USD

$$

A massive monkey mural (the restaurant's namesake is the divine monkey of Hindu and Buddhist traditions) welcomes you to this colorful place with a long bar and a rear patio. The younger sister of the renowned Thip Kao restaurant, which serves a broad menu of highly acclaimed Laotian cuisine, Hanumanh also knows how to blend flavors. The beef larb and the banana-blossom salad alone are worth coming for.

The cocktail list makes creative use of Southeast Asian ingredients. The Som Nam Nah (which translates as "That's what you get...!") has gin, aquavit, lime, ginger, and lemongrass—and an eye-opening touch of bird's-eye chili. The Panda(n) Killer contains soy sauce, to mind-blowingly good effect.

Refreshingly, Hanumanh doesn't take reservations, and just operates on a first-come, first-served basis. But if you come and find a line, know that it's worth the wait.

Maydan

DC hot spot, literally:
A firepit brings on a
cooking frenzy.

1346 Florida Avenue NW

W

maydandc.com

Tues–Sun 5–10:30pm

USD

$$$

Housed in a refurbished historic laundry, Maydan is a smart Middle Eastern gem that as of 2022 was definitely DC's hot spot. This is apt, given the central, open-fire kitchen. Lamb legs hang over the coals, vegetables and flatbreads sizzle on the grill, and chefs hop madly about the flame juggling orders. It's like being at a barbecue-crazed uncle's place for dinner, only these chefs are highly skilled.

Start your visit with a cocktail; I recommend the Chacha Slide. Then peruse the industrial-chic-meets-Mid-East decor of etched glass, greenery, and hanging lamps. And only then decide on your dishes: traditional hummus, kebab, steak, and lamb. All meats are rubbed and cooked with kick-ass spices such as turmeric, fenugreek, za'atar, and Egyptian dukkah. Expect satisfied bellies and burps of contentment.

If you're wanting a feast and no tedious decision-making, opt for the incredible Tawle set menu: course after course of dips and grilled meats or seafood.

Epic Eats

The Red Hen

One of the best modern Italian eateries on the East Coast.

1822 First Street NW

W

theredhendc.com

Mon–Fri 5:30–10pm

Sat & Sun 5–10pm

USD

$$

I can hear the squawks of approval from here. Yes, you'll soon understand why I've sent you to the Red Hen, a genuine neighborhood restaurant in Bloomingdale, on the edge of Shaw.

To start with, reservations are possible, but walk-ins are accepted (yay!), with seats allocated at the communal U-shaped bar or the wooden tables within the warm and rustic brick interior. But the main draw is the food. This is one of the best contemporary Italian (*Italian* Italian, not American Italian) eateries on the East Coast.

Of the perfectly cooked house-made pastas, my go-to is rigatoni with sausage ragu—but everything's good. The ever-changing list of main dishes is brief but spectacular, with the likes of pan-roasted halibut and beef short rib. The Eurocentric wine and craft beers seal the deal.

Before you fly the coop, indulge in a maple panna cotta accompanied by an Italian dessert wine.

The Royal

This café morphs into a cocktail bar and restaurant by night.

---

501 Florida Avenue NW

W

theroyaldc.com

Mon–Thurs 10am–10pm
Fri & Sat 10am–12am
Sun 10am–9pm

USD

$$

This quaint corner café-bar makes you feel like you live down the street, whether you do or not, such is the friendly and casual ambience and delicious food. Its light, airy interior, original terrazzo floors, plants, bookshelves, and bright pictures create a homey atmosphere. There's pleasant outdoor seating too.

The varied menu skews Latin, and the special stars are Colombian-style arepas, chewy corn cakes topped with goodies. The best ones are on the morning menu: chorizo and egg, as well as the cheese-stuffed arepa rancheros, with a fried egg, beans, and avocado. Come lunchtime, a wood oven is fired up, for hanger steak and other meats.

As the Royal is named after the liquor store that occupied this spot for years, it's not surprising that house cocktails are heavy on the rum and aguardiente. Happy hour is 3pm to 6pm Monday to Friday, with $9 cocktails and a few cheap bar snacks.

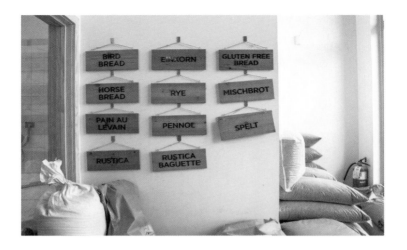

Seylou

DC's best artisanal bakery serves up real-deal pain au levain.

926 N Street NW

W

seylou.com

Wed–Sun 9am–4pm

USD

$

By far DC's best and most authentic bakery, Seylou is filled with the lovely aroma of toasted grains, baked crusts, and roasted coffee.

The owners, Jonathan Bethony and Jessica Azeez, source and buy their wheat, millet, rye, and spelt from farmers in the mid-Atlantic region who use regenerative methods. Every step, from the grinding to baking (in a massive wood-fired oven), is then completed on the premises—in fact, at work stations you see as you enter.

The result is Seylou's bestseller: a simple, chewy pain au levain. But there's also a wide selection of excellent sweet pastries, including millet cookies, pains au raisin, and burnt-sugar canelés. So stock up for a picnic, or sugar-charge yourself for sightseeing.

Supra

Fresh-flavored Georgian food + contemporary setting = satisfying surprise.

———————————————

1205 11th Street NW

W

supradc.com

Mon–Thurs 11:30am–3pm & 5–9pm

Fri 11:30am–3pm & 5–10pm

Sat 10am–3pm & 5–10pm

Sun 10am–3pm & 5–9pm

USD

$$

This sophisticated Georgian restaurant ticks the boxes for quality and authentic cuisine. Its interior is a standout too: modern wooden paneling, a stunning terrazzo floor, and quirky decor, such as hanging traditional hats.

In Georgian, *supra* is the word for a feast accompanied by numerous toasts to family and friends and life. Appropriately, the restaurant is renowned for its list of Georgian wines. And no feast is complete without khachapuri, the signature Georgian bread filled with cheese and a runny egg. Fill out the table with shareable plates such as nigvzit, eggplant slices rolled up with a paste of walnut, garlic, and pomegranate.

The best deal is the three-course, one-hour business lunch for $25. A generous happy hour runs weekdays from 3pm to 7pm, and to 5pm on weekends.

Tiger Fork

Chinese favorites, dim sum, and street food in a hip locale.

922 N Street (Rear) NW

W

tigerforkdc.com

Tues–Thurs & Sun
5–10pm
Fri 5–11pm
Sat 1–11pm

USD
$$

One of DC's most appealing options, tucked away in the historic—and now hip—Blagden Alley, Tiger Fork receives great reviews for the cuisine: fun, contemporary riffs on Chinese favorites, dim sum, and Hong Kong street food. Don't miss the crisp-yet-fatty pork belly or the spicy chili wontons.

It's a dimly lit space with dragon-covered walls and Asian art. You'll need to reserve ahead to score a seat at one of the long communal tables. Or, if you're prepared to wait, grab a seat at the front bar. It whips up cocktails with names such as In the Mood for Love and 8 O'Clock Light Show; the latter claims to combat fatigue—perfect for jet-lagged travelers.

Fancy Radish

Stylish vegan eatery with an attractive bar.

600 H Street NE

W

fancyradishdc.com

Mon & Wed–Fri
5pm–2am
Sat & Sun 5pm–3am

USD

$$

Fancy Radish bills itself simply as a modern vegetable restaurant. It produces the kinds of dishes you'd not necessarily recognize as vegan, such are the creative and tasty results. Some diners even claim it converts ardent carnivores.

The seasonally changing menu has only around 10 items. Main dishes that wow include the spicy dan dan noodles with glazed mushrooms and the Peruvian potatoes, which pop with cilantro, peanuts, and olives. The desserts shine too, especially the sticky toffee pudding. The restaurant's contemporary-look concrete floor and blond-wood furniture complement the up-to-the-minute veggie variations.

It's one of DC's more upmarket vegetarian eateries, but it won't break the bank. Still, if you're on a budget, consider happy hour at the bar (Tuesday to Friday, 5pm to 7pm), for $8 cocktails and tasty $6 bar snacks.

Epic Eats

Maketto

Contemporary community place blending Cambodian and Taiwanese flair and flavors.

1351 H Street NE

W

maketto1351.com

Mon–Sat 9am–10pm

USD

$$

Spearheaded by well-known DC chef Erik Bruner-Yang, Maketto is a vast modern space that sprawls between buildings, with a courtyard, a roof deck, and a catwalk that connects retail, eating, and bar sections. It's an all-things-for-all-people locale, which isn't surprising, given Bruner-Yang's active commitment to community, by supporting food programs in the city and an initiative that helped hospitality workers through the pandemic.

Students and professionals start their days at Maketto over a coffee and pastry. Creative souls and full-on foodies head here for a break and lunch. And everyone seems to stop by for a cocktail. You can even sate your appetite for shopping at the Annex, which is stocked with contemporary streetwear.

And the cuisine? The kitchen serves up a quality mix of Cambodian and Taiwanese flavors, conjuring everything from pork steamed bao to rockfish curry to smoked bison short ribs. It's super-popular; best to reserve for evening meals. It's great for weekend brunch too.

Stable

Swiss tastes, DC-style, and mountains of cheese.

1324 H Street NE

W

stabledc.com

Thurs & Fri 5–9:30pm

Sat 10am–2pm &

5–9:30pm

Sun 10am–2pm

USD

$$

With reclaimed wood paneling and cozy pillows, DC's only American-Swiss eatery recreates the feel of an Alpine lodge, if a small one. And rather than après-ski, the scene is après-work, when folks roll in for an archetypal meal of cheese fondue—good value for two people should you want something filling.

I favor it for après-night-out, though, when the brunch menu's Berner rösti cures all, with crispy potatoes, caramelized onions, bacon, and Gruyère cheese all baked together into a pile of scrumptiousness and topped with a fried egg.

For something sweet, choose from any of the baked goods at the front counter, such as a berliner filled with Toblerone mousse. Drinks, including cocktails, European wines, and kafi schnaps (coffee schnapps) will launch you off the mountain. The only bump on the way down is that the coffees are on the pricier side.

The Duck & the Peach

*Could have attitude,
but doesn't; enjoyable
contemporary vibe.*

---

300 7th Street SE

W

duckandpeachdc.com

Wed–Fri 5–10pm

Sat 10am–3pm & 5–10pm

Sun 10am–3pm

USD

$$$

Hollis Wells Silverman, formerly an executive with legendary DC restaurateur José Andrés, sure knows how to curate spaces. Her first independent effort pops with style: open shelves with coffee-table books, Scandinavian-style chairs, paintings of flowers and landscapes (courtesy of her artist father), and arty designer lighting.

Despite the smart setting, the attitude is easygoing and it sets the tone for equally relaxed dining—a bit like eating a family meal prepared by an experienced chef. The star of the menu is the rotisserie, which turns out juicy, golden-brown organic chicken, Peking duck, and even whole dorade. All these are portioned for two to share; smaller plates include seared scallops and braised beef cheek.

Do note the uncommon approach to service: For every party, large or small, 22 percent is added to the check, "to help professionalize pay in the restaurant industry"—essentially a mandated tip, so servers earn a more reliable wage, and you don't need to add more.

Pluma

Made-from-scratch bakery with DC's best croissants.

391 Morse Street NE

plumabybluebird.com

Tues–Thurs 7am–5pm
Fri 7am–7pm
Sat & Sun 8am–7pm

USD
$

Pluma is a love letter to baked goods. In fact, the husband-and-wife team met over their passion for baking. They run both Bluebird Bakery (which supplies other cafés) as well as the on-site café Pluma, a small space with a communal table, for lucky customers to get the goods hot from the oven.

The chocolate-pistachio croissant is one of the best this side of Paris (if indeed France would dare such a risqué combination). For something a bit more substantial, try one of the interesting sweet snacks, such as ricotta toast with honey and fennel pollen, or a savory breakfast sandwich of pork belly, cheddar, and egg on brioche, or a classic croque madame. One nice extra: A gluten-free option, such as a seasonal buckwheat cake, is always offered. A full coffee and tea menu seals the deal.

The District Fishwife

Super-fresh seafood you'll want to shout about.

1309 5th Street NE

W

thedistrictfishwife.com

Mon–Sun 10am–6pm

USD

$$

Fiona Lewis, the Australian American owner of this seafood shop and counter-service restaurant in Union Market, named her place with her tongue firmly in cheek. She is hardly the fishwife of old—when the word implied a shouting nag—but DC's only female fishmonger, who's also a nationally recognized expert on sustainable seafood and conservation of all things aquatic. And no one would blame Lewis for boasting loudly about her wares, as it's all impeccably fresh and sourced almost entirely from the East Coast.

This is a great lunch stop for fish and chips or a salmon burger, served with some of the best fries around. The poke is also excellent, showcasing excellent fish you won't worry about eating raw. Net them all early, as these swim out the door.

Lewis also runs two sister eateries in Union Market: On Toast, for all things tasty served, yes, on toast, and Son of a Fish, with sushi and sashimi boxes that are of course the freshest around.

St. Anselm

*Top American tavern
with great food and
vibey atmosphere.*

1250 5th Street NE

W

stanselmdc.com

Mon–Thurs 5–10pm
Fri 12pm–3pm & 5–11pm
Sat 10:30am–11pm
Sun 10:30am–10pm

USD

$$

First opened in Brooklyn in 2011, St. Anselm is a sort of faux-old-school American tavern. This second location, opened in 2018 by Starr Restaurant Group (Le Diplomate, see p.129), brought the same aesthetic of dark wood, carpets, and taxidermy to the Union Market District. The place has been a success thanks to its moody interior (love those cozy lamps on the banquette tables), but also because the service is consistently good, the '70s playlist is fun, and the steakhouse menu and European-focused wine list are both excellent.

It's all about grilled goodies here, in small and large portions. The 16-ounce rib eye is justifiably popular, but for me, the salmon collar with lemon and garlic butter triumphs. And the buttermilk biscuits with pimento cheese alone are worth going for.

Reserve ahead for the 120-seat dining room, or try your luck for places at the chef's counter or the U-shaped bar. There's limited patio seating too.

Union Market

*This renovated city market is a magnet
for food lovers.*

The '60s-concrete Union Market building doesn't look like much on the outside, but inside it's lined with more than 30 food stalls—a fun place for lunch before hitting the stores in the surrounding streets of this revitalized wholesale area.

In the market building, you can grab anything from a slice of American pizza to bowls of Chinese dumplings. I may be biased, but Australian-owned The District Fishwife (see p.144), a sustainable seafood venture, is my favorite for its range of delectable dishes to go. A branch of Immigrant Food (also at Planet Word, p.178) serves up the best Cuban sandwich this side of Havana. And if you've not yet been to Lucky Buns (see p.76) in Adams Morgan, not to worry: You have a chance to try their highly reputed burgers here. There's seating inside and at picnic tables outside. Though fair warning: Visitors flock to the market on weekends, and service can be slow as a result.

Beyond the eating options, homeware stores also display stylish wares. And on top of it all—literally—is Hi-Lawn, an ultra-casual, expansive bar that covers the building's entire rooftop. It's open every evening, and earlier Friday through Sunday, all weather permitting.

1309 5th Street NE

W

unionmarketdc.com

Mon–Sat 8am–9pm
Sun 8am–8pm

Epic Eats

FEDERAL FREEBIES

*A great treat, perhaps the greatest treat of Washington, DC:
To enjoy this capital requires very little capital, at least when
it comes to culture. Whether through world-class art at the
National Gallery or American democracy at the Capitol,
the city is yours to explore for next to nothing.*

*Any visitor to DC should thank geologist James
Smithson, whose fortune established the Smithsonian
Institution (see p.151), a wondrous network of 19 museums
and galleries, 13 gardens, the National Zoo, and numerous
research centers. And every one in DC is free.*

*On top of that are several other blockbuster collections,
equally free and equally captivating, not to mention loads
of free arts programming (for venues with both paid and
free entertainment, such as the Kennedy Center, see the next
chapter, p.173). In fact, there are so many free attractions
that I can offer only my top picks, a mere fraction of what's
on view. I hope they give you both pleasure and insight into
DC, the US, and the world.*

The Castle at the Smithsonian

The first outpost of the Smithsonian Institution, and still its heart.

Looking very much like a place of learning and wisdom—or, depending on your frame of reference, straight out of a scene from *Harry Potter*—the Castle opened in 1855 as the first Smithsonian Institution. It typically functions as the visitor center, where volunteer staff can quiz you on your interests and help you plan your day.

Unfortunately, at the time of going to print in 2023, the building had just closed for its first major renovation in more than 50 years, and the extensive works are anticipated to last until 2028. During this time, the Smithsonian's Visitor Center will operate online, and there are plans to install temporary visitor facilities near the castle. Still, it's worth popping by, just to see the building, as well as the adjoining Enid A. Haupt Garden.

1000 Jefferson Drive SW

si.edu

Mon–Sun
8:30am–5:30pm

THE WHO AND WHAT OF THE SMITHSONIAN INSTITUTION

Smithsonian founder James Smithson was born in Paris in 1765, the illegitimate son of a wealthy British widow and her lover, the first Duke of Northumberland. For his education, Smithson moved to Great Britain, but he was never afforded the full rights of a British citizen. He graduated from Oxford University and became known for his scientific studies in chemistry and geology.

Never married and with no children, Smithson willed his substantial fortune to a nephew, with the stipulation that if the nephew had no heirs, the money would then go to the US government, to create "an establishment for the increase and diffusion of knowledge." Indeed, the nephew died childless six years later, and thus the Smithsonian Institution was born. With this funding, the US government has created and maintains (along with support from private donors) a wide-range of museums, galleries and sites which visitors are able to access for free.

In his whole wide-ranging life, Smithson never set foot on US soil; perhaps the gift was meant as a snub to Great Britain. In death, though, he did arrive: In 1904, his body was shipped from Italy and later installed in a crypt by the front entrance.

SMITHSONIAN MUSEUMS

Anacostia Community Museum
Arts and Industries Building
Cooper Hewitt, Smithsonian Design Museum (New York)
Hirshhorn Museum and Sculpture Garden (see p.154)
National Air and Space Museum
National Air and Space Museum's Steven F. Udvar-Hazy Center
   (Chantilly, Virginia)
National Museum of African American History & Culture (see p.160)
National Museum of African Art
National Museum of American History (see p.162)
National Museum of Asian Art
National Museum of Natural History (see p.163)
National Museum of the American Indian
National Museum of the American Indian's George Gustav Heye Center
   (New York City)
National Portrait Gallery (see p.167)
National Postal Museum
Smithsonian American Art Museum (see National Portrait Gallery)
Smithsonian's National Zoo and Conservation Biology Institute
The Castle at the Smithsonian (see p.151)

In December 2020 Congress passed to establish two new Smithsonian
museums, the National Museum of the American Latino (currently a
dedicated gallery in the National Museum of American History, while the
separate museum is being built) and the Smithsonian American Women's
History Museum, still in development.

Hirshhorn Museum

Eye-catching contemporary art installations in a modernist landmark building.

Independence Avenue SW
and 7th Street SW

W

hirshhorn.si.edu

Mon–Sun 10am–5:30pm

Hirshhorn building is impossible to miss: a hollow-centered cylinder, designed by Pritzker Prize–winning architect Gordon Bunshaft, that's a modernist artwork in its own right. The gallery showcases modern art of all mediums drawn from a collection of 12,000 pieces, as well as curated exhibitions by some of the world's leading contemporary artists.

Over three levels, you can get your head around artworks as you follow the building's curves. A vast temporary exhibition space houses immersive art experiences, which have included installations by Ai Weiwei and, more recently, *One With Eternity*, a survey of spellbinding work by visionary artist Yayoi Kusama.

The lobby, redesigned by Japanese artist Hiroshi Sugimoto and opened in 2018, has a café, Dolcezza at the Hirshhorn (p.44).

After you've grabbed a coffee, cross Jefferson Drive to the four acres of the sunken sculpture garden to contemplate around 30 works by Auguste Rodin, Henry Moore, and more.

Library of Congress
Thomas Jefferson Building

The main building of America's largest library speaks volumes about DC and the nation.

---

10 First Street SE

W

loc.gov

Tues–Sat 8:30am–5pm

Near the Capitol, and linked to it by an underground tunnel, the Library of Congress occupies three buildings crammed with more than 164 million items—or put another way: 838 miles (1,349km) of shelves of books, maps, photographs, and manuscripts. For visitors, the beautiful Italian Renaissance-style Thomas Jefferson Building is the main attraction, with its marble floors, stained glass, cherubs, busts, and allegorical murals. It was constructed between 1888 and 1897 to house Jefferson's books, which he donated after the British had burned the Capitol, where the original library was located, in 1814.

You can see the replica of Jefferson's library, along with many of the original books. You can also eyeball two 1450s Bibles from Germany: the handwritten Giant Bible of Mainz and the Gutenberg Bible. Another highlight is the main reading room and its masterful dome.

Lincoln Memorial

*Ode to Lincoln and a
temple in many respects.*

2 Lincoln Memorial Circle NW

W

nps.gov/linc

24 hrs

At the far west end of the National Mall, the
Lincoln Memorial is perhaps the capital's
most symbolic monument, and hard to beat
for its meaning, scale, and vistas. Henry
Bacon designed this impressive Doric temple,
which was completed in 1912, while Daniel
Chester carved the 19-foot-tall (5.8m) statue
of Abraham Lincoln himself. The 36 columns
represent the number of states at the time
of the president's death. On the side walls
are inscribed his famous Gettysburg Address
(south), in which he resolved that Civil War
deaths would not be in vain, and his second
Inaugural Address (north), which called for
postwar compassion, "to bind the nation's
wounds." On the stairs leading up to the
memorial, 18 steps from the top, a marker
shows where Dr. Martin Luther King Jr. stood
in 1963 to deliver his famous "I Have a
Dream" speech.

The best time to visit the memorial
is at night, when it's lit up and there are
few other visitors. Follow Lincoln's gaze out
over the reflecting pool, and you'll have an
entrancing view of the whole city laid out
before you.

National Archives Museum

*Keeping records of how it
all begin in the USA.*

---

701 Constitution Avenue NW

museum.archives.gov

Mon–Sun 10am–5:30pm

Here, in this grand neoclassical building,
you can eyeball the essential paperwork of
American democracy, the documents that
make the country tick. First and foremost
is the original Declaration of Independence,
signed by 56 delegates, including John
Hancock, whose space-hogging flourish
has made his name into American slang
for a signature. The other two stars: the
US Constitution and the Bill of Rights.

But to my mind, the real fun is in the
interactive exhibits in the public vaults and
the David M. Rubenstein Gallery, beyond the
dimly lit rotunda. I'm talking rooms crammed
with items to open, investigate, watch, and
read. You can pore over Abraham Lincoln's
telegrams and pick up a proper old telephone
(yes, with a dial!) to eavesdrop on President
Nixon's Oval Office conversations. The
Rubenstein Gallery focuses on the evolution
of rights—speech, equality, religion—and has
some fascinating video footage of civil-rights
protests and anti-war demonstrations. It even
holds one of the four surviving originals of
the 1297 Magna Carta, the British document
that served as a model for American liberty.

National Gallery of Art

*Extraordinary world masterpieces spread across two
design-focused buildings.*

This amazing gallery consists of the neoclassical West Building (enter at
6th Street) and the I.M. Pei-designed East Building (enter at 4th Street).
Befitting for each architectural style, the West Building holds older European
art, up to the cusp of modernism, from Da Vinci to Van Gogh, while the
East Building showcases modern art, starting with a massive Calder mobile
suspended in the lobby.

Given the gallery's size and scope, the only problem is how to tackle it.
Don't try to do it all in one visit. Just grab a map from reception and cherry-
pick by theme or year or artist. My personal favorites include Picasso's *Family
of Saltimbanques* and Pollock's *Number 1, 1950 (Lavender Mist)*, as well as the
room full of Rothkos, where, amazingly, I often have the whole place to myself.
Architecture fans may wish to simply wander through the buildings. But be
sure to go through the underground walkway that connects the two buildings:
It's ignited by Leo Villareal's dazzling light sculpture *Multiverse*.

Excellent volunteer tours are available, and check the website for the
schedule of free talks and screenings, especially on weekends. When you're
done (for now), rest up in the sculpture garden, where a pleasant café serves
beer and wine.

Constitution Avenue NW   nga.gov   Mon–Sun 10am–5pm

National Museum of African American History & Culture

Time for only one DC museum? This. Is. It.

Clad in striking ornamental bronze-colored lattice, the unmissable museum building houses exhibits about the African American experience, from before the nation existed up through contemporary times. The route proceeds chronologically from the ground floor, where you enter first into the sobering Slavery and Freedom area. The windowless space can feel claustrophobic, particularly if it's crowded, but this intentionally evokes the sensation of being in the hold of a slave ship.

As you wind your way up the levels, the tone lightens a bit. You come face to face with celebrated sports folk, musicians, and artists via high-tech screens and interactive exhibits. Don't miss Carl Lewis's track shoes, life-size hip-hop performers, and Chuck Berry's Cadillac. The entire museum experience encompasses facets of an essential American story and culture that continues to change over time.

The museum opened in 2016 and is still deservedly popular, so it's wise to reserve a timed-entry pass online. Alternatively, try for one of the daily tickets, released online at 8:15am weekdays.

1400 Constitution
Avenue NW

nmaahc.si.edu

Mon–Sun 10am–5:30pm
(last entry 4pm)

National Museum of American History

The place to come for nostalgia, artifacts, and all things American.

Constitution Avenue NW
(between 12th and
14th Streets)

W

americanhistory.si.edu

Mon–Sun 10am–5:30pm

This is the spot that salvages and preserves the cultural, political, and social history of the United States, in the form of more than 1.7 million objects, not to mention 22,000 linear feet (6,706m) of archival documents.

Obviously not all of this can be shown at once, so exhibits rotate. What you *might* see: Dorothy's ruby slippers from *The Wizard of Oz*, Julia Child's kitchen, and great dresses worn by first ladies. Hanging in the main lobby is a modern representation of the flag that flew over Baltimore's Fort McHenry during the War of 1812—that is, the star-spangled banner that inspired Francis Scott Key to write what became the national anthem. A gallery to the right of here houses the real thing.

For people steeped in American pop culture, the museum provides a trip down memory lane. But even if you're less well versed, or just less nostalgic, you can simply marvel at the sheer range of quirky items: So that's where Lincoln's stovepipe hat ended up!

National Museum of Natural History

DC's most visited museum has something for everyone.

10th Street NW and
Constitution Avenue NW

W

naturalhistory.si.edu

Mon–Sun 10am–5:30pm

The Natural History Museum is a favorite for kids and kids at heart. It's so crammed with stuff that it's hard to suggest highlights—there's something for everyone. One literally big draw is the massive *Tyrannosaurus rex* skeleton that lords over the dinosaur hall. A small butterfly pavilion (a rare extra charge) draws in the juniors, while adults tend to home in on the megalodon jaws and the fossil lab on the first floor. Anyone with a morbid streak will like the Egyptian mummies on the second floor. And among the (again, literal) gems is the Hope Diamond, the largest cut blue diamond known in the world.

One quirk of navigation: You can't walk all the way around the rotunda, so must retrace your steps or use an elevator. Consider it opportunity to acknowledge the (yes, literal!) elephant in the room: Henry, 11 tons of taxidermy that's been on display in the center of the rotunda, and lovingly cared for, since 1959.

US Capitol

Center of the US government.
And a very grand building besides.

A tour around the Capitol is essential to any DC visit. This is where it all happens. Congress. House of Representatives. The Senate. Famous busts. The starting point for DC's street system (take the tour; you'll see what I mean). And yes, site of the incursion of January 6, 2021.

Visits start with a rather cheesy and patriotic 13-minute film, then a volunteer guide takes you through various spaces: a vaulted "crypt" (named for its resemblance to a church crypt; no one is buried here); the Capitol Rotunda, crowned with the 4,664-square-foot (433 sq m) fresco *The Apotheosis of Washington*, depicting the first president in godlike glory; and the Greek-revival-style National Statuary Hall, which displays gift statues from the 50 states. Occasionally, you'll see members of Congress wandering around, identifiable by their lapel pins.

After the tour, you're free to explore the fabulous exhibits in the vast underground visitor center. Learn about the functions of Congress and the history of the building itself, from its first construction in 1793, to its 1814 burning by the British, and through several later extensions and restorations. There's also a cafeteria if you find yourself peckish.

Ordinarily, visitors are also welcome to sit in the galleries of the Senate and the House and watch Congress in session, but as of late 2022, this was still temporarily suspended. When it's reinstated, check in with the House and Senate appointments desks on the upper level. Foreign visitors must show a passport.

First Street SE   visitthecapitol.gov   Mon–Fri 9am–3pm

Washington Monument

*Experience DC's lofty
status from its most
visible landmark.*

The Mall

nps.gov/wamo

Mon–Sun 9am–5pm
(last tour at 4pm)

This slender 555ft (169m) obelisk was for a time the world's tallest structure—until the Eiffel Tower—twice as tall!—was completed in 1889. Still, though, thanks to height-limit laws passed in the late 19th and early 20th centuries, the Monument still towers over DC. Construction on the marble obelisk, meant to commemorate George Washington, began in 1848, but it was halted during the Civil War. When the work restarted, different marble was used. Look closely about one-third of the way up: You can see the two distinct colors of stone.

For awesome 360-degree views of the city, an ear-popping elevator ride zooms you to the top, where there are also exhibits about the obelisk's history.

Entry is free, but tickets are required. Book online up to 30 days in advance; a limited number of tickets are held for 24-hour-advance reservations, available at 10am for the next day's time slots. Failing all that, try for a same-day walk-up ticket at the Washington Monument Lodge (15th Street between Madison and Jefferson Drives); try to arrive before it opens at 8:45am.

National Portrait Gallery

Come face to face with past presidents and many others.

8th Street NW and
G Street NW

W

npg.si.edu

Mon–Sun 11:30am–7pm

Technically, this city-block-size building holds two Smithsonian museums, the National Portrait Gallery and the American Art Museum (americanart.si.edu), though effectively they run together inside, and most visitors come for the America's Presidents gallery, on the second floor. Here hang 44 (the 45th is still in process) specially commissioned official portraits of presidents, along with first ladies, beginning with Hillary Clinton. Not only will you see the familiar faces that grace American money—George Washington by Gilbert Stuart, for instance—but you'll see a fascinating shift in painting styles and formality over the centuries, from the lace collars of yore to the vivid colors of Barack and Michelle Obama (though these, by Kehinde Wiley, are often out on loan).

From the portrait gallery, head to the third floor for classic American artwork by Roy Lichtenstein and Andy Warhol or to the first for Edward Hopper and Georgia O'Keeffe. The folk-art gallery includes some extraordinary pieces by African American artists.

District Wharf

Happening waterfront destination with
bars, entertainment, and more.

Opened in 2017, the Wharf is one of DC's development success stories. On the banks of Washington Channel, an offshoot of the Potomac River, what used to be a fish market and warehouses is now a large complex of apartments, offices, shops, hotels, and restaurants. In fact, development continues: As of 2022, the second phase, an extension east as far as Nationals Park was nearing completion.

I usually head to the Wharf on a weekend, as it has good public space for mingling and relaxed entertainment venues. As for sights, the Wharf *is* the destination, with pleasant water views and a scenic promenade and marina.

The area is especially lovely at sunset, when you can enjoy a drink on a terrace or rooftop at one of the area's many bars. It's also home to The Anthem, one of DC's more cutting-edge performance spaces, as well as the fabulous Pearl Street Warehouse, an intimate and more indie-focused bar and venue. Definitely check out what's playing at both.

In terms of wandering? Go for it; it's easy to get around. Follow the promenade and its several perpendicular lanes. My morning visits start with a café con leche at Colada Shop, sister to the one on 14th Street (see p.53). Browse in a branch of Politics and Prose (see p.202), a wonderful bookshop with a great author program and up-to-the-minute stock. A good option for casual lunch is Bistro du Jour, a French brasserie that offers a little of everything, from pastries to cocktails and larger French-focused dishes. On your meander, jump on a swing on Recreation Pier (and possibly pose for a photo; everyone else is doing it!). Or grab a stick and a marshmallow at Camp Wharf, an Airstream trailer on the promenade and, for around $4, make your own s'mores at the firepit.

For afternoons and evenings, the smart Whiskey Charlie (whiskeycharliewharf.com) has a wonderful roof terrace above the Canopy hotel, and it delivers a solid cocktail menu along with impressive vistas. Or settle in at the more casual Cantina Bambina, dockside, for a strong margarita. For dinner, the Wharf is packed with smart places—but you don't come here for a cheap night out. Del Mar does high-end seafood, while Moon Rabbit is the most popular among foodies (and it's better value). The Vietnamese American owner whips up classic Vietnamese dishes with an American spin.

Don't be daunted by the Wharf's position on a map. The overpass of the Dwight D. Eisenhower Freeway, which borders the Wharf on the north side, looks impassable, but in fact from the Smithsonian Castle, it's only a 20-minute walk; head south along L'Enfant Plaza (7th Street SW), and the route heads right over the freeway. For Metro riders, the central promenade is a 10-minute walk northwest from the Waterfront station on the Green line (or a 15-minute walk from L'Enfant Plaza, served by five lines). And a free shuttle operates from the Mall to the Wharf via 7th Street, then back via 10th Street.

760 Maine Ave SW

W

thewharfdc.com

Mon–Sun 24 hours

WALLET WORTHY

With his generosity, James Smithson created one big problem for DC (or at least for me): Given all the extraordinary collections in the free Smithsonian museums, it might be difficult to convince you that sometimes it's worth—shock! horror!—paying up.

But the city does have some fabulous theaters and other attractions that are worth the price of entry. I'm not talking about emptying your purse, but for a perfectly reasonable fee, you can snoop in the International Spy Museum (p.175; the hidden camera in the cigarette lighter is worth the price of admission!) or explore the dizzying visuals of Artechouse (see p.174). Then there are performance spaces galore, where you can shell out as little as $10—or multiples of $100. The Kennedy Center (see p.177) is the biggest name, but check out other independent theaters and stages for thought-provoking contemporary plays and great live bands. These include the Arena in Navy Yard, The Anthem at District Wharf (see p.169), and Studio Theater on 14th Street.

Artechouse

Stimulate your senses in this experience that's off the usual DC spectrum.

1238 Maryland Avenue SW

W

artechouse.com

Mon–Sun 10am–9:15pm
(with other varied
exhibition hours)

USD

Tickets from $25

One of three such venues in the US, Artechouse is an experience—specifically an experience that uses technology to create interactive art. You, the viewer, are called upon to immerse yourself in and sometimes influence what you see around you on giant video projections and screens. You might find yourself waving your arms to create new shapes and colors, or flopped on a beanbag to absorb stimulating lights and sounds.

The exhibit changes from time to time. Past exhibitions have included *Life of a Neuron*, in which visitors lost themselves in the workings of the body at a cellular level. In *Transient: Impermanent Paintings*, visitors played with virtual brushstrokes and musical notes to create imagined landscapes with unique soundtracks. No matter what's on when you visit, it's bound to be vivid and stimulating. (Though likely *too* stimulating for anyone with light sensitivities.)

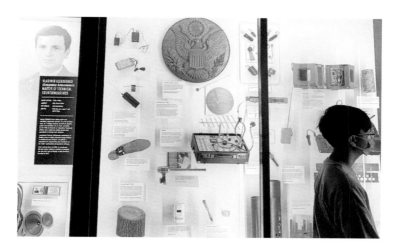

International Spy Museum

Uncover secrets, espionage, and your alter-ego spy.

700 L'Enfant Plaza

W

spymuseum.org

Mon–Sun 9am–7pm

USD

Adults $27, Children $17

Admittedly you need to be a bit spy-obsessed to justify the admission price, but if the subject piques your interest, commit to the experience fully: Reserve tickets ahead and log in at the website to receive your cover identity. You're welcomed with a hearty "Good luck on your mission, Agent!" and set loose in the fun-filled and very interesting museum. I recommend two to three hours to do justice to all the "shadow world" details crammed in the two floors, in sections on codes, secrets, and covert actions—some of which test your spy skills through questions and puzzles. The high-tech exhibits cover nifty gadgets, such as the hidden cameras and microphones used by intelligence agencies around the world.

But it's not all fun and games. In fact, quite the opposite. Accounts of the job from real-life spies and major international spy operations, from the Stasi of East Germany to Israel, keep it real. And the information on assassinations and state-sponsored torture hits hard, but should make visitors think and encourage debate.

John F. Kennedy Center for the Performing Arts

Iconic DC site and vibrant theater and artistic space.

The idea of a national theater—much needed in this politically focused city—started with Eleanor Roosevelt in the 1930s. Funds were earmarked under President Eisenhower, and President Kennedy kick-started construction. Opened in 1971, the white minimalist monolith, designed by Edward Durell Stone, is a kind of living memorial to JFK, as well as a DC icon.

Big-name acts and dancers grace the three main stages: a 2,456-seat concert hall, plus a chandelier-bedecked opera house and the Eisenhower Theater. Musicals often head here from London's West End or Broadway, and if you're here before Christmas, join loyal DC residents at the Washington Ballet's production of *The Nutcracker*. For free entertainment (aside from admiring the architecture), check the schedule for the Millennial Stage, within the red-carpeted main foyer, where singers and poets perform nightly for free under some oh-so-'60s chandeliers.

In September 2019, three new pavilions with rehearsal and teaching rooms opened, along with a café and landscaped public space. A rooftop bar provides great views across the Potomac.

Although the center is not far from downtown, a spaghetti tangle of highways blocks foot access, except from Georgetown: Walk along the Potomac River trail. Otherwise, catch a free shuttle bus (frequently, 9:45am to midnight, Sundays from 11:45am) from Foggy Bottom Metro station.

📍
2700 F Street NW

🕑
Performance times vary

USD
$0–$960

W
kennedy-center.org

Planet Word

*Tribute to human language at a museum
in a 19th-century school.*

Spread over several floors, the ten or so exhibit spaces are playful and kid-friendly, though equally appealing to adult word nerds as they cover everything from obscure etymologies to the use of language in jokes, music, and advertising.

Many displays are gamelike and voice activated (though a bit biased toward American accents). You'll shout into microphones, sing song lyrics, and stand under the massive globe and call up recordings of individuals from around the world who tell you about their languages. There are also fabulous scenes of babies grappling with language. At the museum's heart is a beautiful library, also featuring small dioramas of scenes from well-known children's books (I won't spoil the surprise!).

You'll also find a wonderful word-themed gift shop and an excellent restaurant, Immigrant Food, with a menu of fusion cuisine, such as a Vietnamese banh mi with a Caribbean twist, or Madam VP's Heritage Bowl, a curry-and-rice meal that nods to Kamala Harris's Indian and Jamaican heritage.

925 13th Street NW

Wed–Sun 10am–5pm

USD

Entry $15
(suggested donation)

planetwordmuseum.org

Dumbarton Oaks Gardens

*Experience living history at this landscaped garden
and museum.*

Dumbarton Oaks estate was the home of John and Mildred Bliss, keen and wealthy travelers (John was a diplomat). In 1921, they hired Beatrice Farrand to design the gardens. A prominent landscape architect, Farrand had previously helped design First Lady Edith Wilson's garden at the White House, as well as botanic gardens at Princeton and Yale. Farrand and Mildred Bliss became friends and collaborators on Dumbarton Oaks' 16 acres, and they worked together for 30 years—even well after the Blisses gifted their entire property to Harvard University and downsized to a smaller home elsewhere in Georgetown.

Part of the house—including a cutting-edge addition—functions as a museum to display the Blisses' extraordinary art collection, mainly pre-Columbian and Byzantine, that they amassed on their journeys. Entrance to the museum (on 32nd Street) and the gardens (on R Street) are separate, and garden tickets must be purchased online.

---

101 R Street NW

W
doaks.org/visit

Museum Tues–Sun
11:30am–5:30pm

Gardens mid-March–Oct
Tues–Sun 2–6pm

USD

Museum free
Gardens $9

Blues Alley

Jazz tunes, fun, and rhythms in the quintessential, intimate club.

1073 Wisconsin Avenue NW

W

bluesalley.com

Mon–Sun from 6pm
(dinner); performances
at 7pm and 9pm

USD

From $30

"Now *this* is a jazz club," iconic trumpeter Dizzy Gillespie reportedly said of Blues Alley. It's still the case. Open since 1965 in a brick carriage house in a lane off Wisconsin Avenue, Blues Alley is a place where you can get up close and personal with performers on the small stage. And just like it was when Gillespie was birthing bebop, DC is still a key stop on the jazz circuit, so anyone who's anyone (or about to be anyone) plays here.

The list of famous people who've graced the stage on their way up include DC native Eva Cassidy and Virginia-born Ella Fitzgerald. Ticket prices are reasonable, but factor in an additional $15 food-or-drink minimum. The menu includes Creole and Cajun classics like blackened catfish and jambalaya studded with andouille.

Georgetown Heritage Canal Boat

Learn about shipping history on a pleasant boat ride on DC's iconic C&O canal.

C&O Lock 3
Thomas Jefferson Street
NW and 30th Street NW

W

georgetownheritage.org

Departures Wed–Sun
10am, 12pm, 2pm & 4pm

USD

One-hour tour $20

Climb aboard to putt along slowly for a mile of the Chesapeake & Ohio Canal. As you go, a tour guide covers the interesting history and technology of the locks—one of which you pass through—and the tales of local folk in the late 1800s. George Washington was the first to envision a canal linking the Potomac to the Ohio River valley. By the time it was completed in 1850, the canal stretched 184.5 miles (297km) to Cumberland, Maryland, and for 100 years it was a transportation method for lumber, coal, and agricultural cargo, as well as passengers—all on boats like the one you're on, but pulled along by harnessed mules. Railways replaced canals, though, and the C&O closed in 1924 following a flood.

Overall, the outing is pleasant, informative, and surprisingly uncheesy, even on a summer weekend, when workers at the locks are outfitted in 19th-century dress. If you don't take the boat, at least take a walk along the canal path, as many locals do. Or ride a bike: The whole route to Maryland takes between three and seven days.

C&O Lock 3 is on the canal towpath near Baked & Wired (see p.47).

Tudor Place

Historic estate reflecting DC's society and
unique architecture.

One of DC's best-preserved estates, this neoclassical mansion is surrounded by 5.5 acres of lawns and gardens. It's worth a visit for aesthetic pleasures—interesting architecture, gorgeous roses—but also for a sense of the complex society in the District during the budding Republic and beyond.

This complexity starts at the outset of each tour, with an acknowledgment of the fact that the owners of Tudor Place, built in 1816, were also owners of human beings—and, as the volunteer guides say, an attempt to "look this injustice in the eye."

These owners were Thomas and Martha Peter, the latter being George Washington's granddaughter. The house remained in the Peter family until the fourth owner, Armistead Peter III, deeded the estate after his death in 1983 to a private foundation. According to his wishes, the house is maintained as a home, not merely a museum, and roughly as he left it. That means antique furniture from all eras—including a 1970s telephone in his intact office, which is crammed with memorabilia—as well as some 200 items once owned by George Washington.

The tour also covers the many stages of the building's design and construction. The pièce de résistance is the extraordinary marble-floored temple portico, the only known example in a US residence, and the only one still standing today.

Tickets must be reserved online ahead of time, and after the tour you're free to wander in the garden.

📍
1644 31st Street NW

🕐
Wed–Sat 10am–4pm
Sun 12pm–4pm

USD
$10

W
tudorplace.org

9:30 Club

*Where any serious
rock-and-roller goes.*

---

815 V Street NW

W

930.com

Performance times vary

USD

Tickets $22–40

So many legendary punk venues have closed, but the 9:30 Club has been rocking hard since 1980 and shows no signs of stopping. An early incubator for DC hardcore bands like Bad Brains and Minor Threat, it has also hosted Nirvana, the Red Hot Chili Peppers, Public Enemy, and Black Flag—all before they got huge (or "sold out," depending on your Gen X perspective). It ranks high on music-media lists of America's best clubs and continues to showcase the famous and those on the rise. Up to a thousand people can pack in here for standing-room shows.

Given the caliber of performers, it's worth checking out the schedule before your trip and buying tickets ahead—though sometimes they're still available at the door. Headline acts typically come on around 10:30pm or later. Four bars tend to the thirsty masses.

Atlas Performing Arts Center

Nonprofit theater that supports Black performers.

1333 H Street NE

W

atlasarts.org

Mon–Sun 11am–5pm
(box office)

USD

Tickets from $35

This iconic retro building—opened as a cinema in 1938—is host to a schedule of award-winning and topical plays, musical acts, and performances of all kinds. Compared with the larger theaters, ticket prices are very accessible, and proceeds go to the nonprofit enterprise.

That's not surprising, given its dramatic background. For decades, the Atlas was one of only four movie theaters in DC. It was destroyed in the 1968 riots, then sat empty for more than 30 years. In 2001, a local philanthropist helped to revive the theater, which then became an anchor for the revitalization of the rest of H Street.

The Atlas has four performance spaces and rents these to artist groups for their own productions, so events can vary wildly. The theater also partners with Capital City Symphony, Mosaic Theater Company of DC, Joy of Motion Dance Center, City at Peace, and Step Afrika!, all of which put on regular shows.

CAPITAL
COMMODITIES

To be blunt: DC isn't a shopping hot spot, at least not for clothing. Fashion tastes skew mainstream and buttoned-up: chinos or tailored Jackie O frocks. When it comes to nifty gifts and tasteful souvenirs, though, there's a bounty in every museum store. You can pick up a great kids' puzzle at the National Building Museum Gift Shop (see p. 191) and artistic designs from the lovely collection in the National Gallery of Art Gift Shop (see p. 190). Even the stunning museum at Dumbarton Oaks Gardens (see p. 181) has gorgeous offerings inspired by its pre-Columbian collection. Independent stores such as Made in DC (see p. 193) support local designers and sell creative cards and beautiful District-themed goods. The White House Visitor Center sells all things political, in a tasteful, across-the-spectrum way, but for tongue-in-cheek takes, look no further than The Outrage (see p. 198).

National Gallery
of Art Gift Shop

Take your favorite art pieces home and work them into your daily lilfe.

6th Street NW and
Constitution Avenue NW

W
shop.nga.gov

Mon–Sun 10am–5pm

Whether or not you've wandered through the two buildings of the National Gallery, you're welcome at this massive gift shop, located on the ground floor of the West Building. The artworks of the world's contemporary and old masters are recreated across a range of items that are perfect for presents, from the sublime (stunning jewelry inspired by Alexander Calder) to the pleasantly ridiculous (a mug with a pixelated image of Frida Kahlo). There's Monet's *Japanese Footbridge* on a watch, Vermeer on note cards, and just about every artist in gorgeous art books. Then there's jigsaw puzzles, scarves, posters, and tote bags. Journals, T-shirts, coloring books, and umbrellas. Fabulous kids' games might encourage learning and art appreciation. The I.M. Pei Wing (the East Building) has a smaller shop that showcases 20th- and 21st-century artists.

National Building Museum Gift Shop

Design-forward gifts minus the kitsch in a Presidential site.

401 F Street NW

nbm.org

Thurs–Mon 11am–4pm

Built between 1882 and 1887, what's now the National Building Museum was originally the headquarters of the US Pension Bureau and a memorial to Civil War Unionists. It has also been the site of numerous presidential inaugurations. After all, this grand, four-story space is impressive, thanks to its Italian Renaissance design: a massive atrium, Corinthian columns, and ornamented balconies. These days, architectural and design exhibitions fill its space, along with temporary events, from avant-garde performances to Shakespeare productions.

But what visitors are often surprised by is the gift shop, which stocks some of the most creative, design-themed gifts in the city. Frank Lloyd Wright–related items are big: You could outfit yourself with Wright head to toe, from patterned hats to jazzy socks. Otherwise, you can fill your suitcase with architecture books, gorgeous cards (art deco motifs of DC, say), high-design home gizmos, and quality toys and puzzles.

Capital Commodities

Made in DC

Stylish one-stop shop for gifts with a DC pedigree.

This charming store has four locations, and this one in Georgetown is handy for working into a larger stroll. The stock brings a much-needed hip element to the city's otherwise chain-driven shopping experience. Step inside to find the work of local creatives who craft, print, carve, and stitch unique pieces. This is the spot to grab a tasteful gift, whether you want something that's clearly DC-themed or simply lovely, with plenty of items that easily fit into a suitcase, such as stationery, jewelry, and candles. Stock is ever changing, but particularly like the illustrated maps of Washington, DC neighborhoods and the beautiful handmade soaps.

1353 Wisconsin Avenue NW

W
shopmadeindc.com

Mon–Sun 11am–7pm

Miss Pixie's

Retro glory: trash, treasure, and everything in between.

1626 14th Street NW

misspixies.com

Mon–Sun 11am–6:30pm

A former car dealership that has been covered in a coat of pink paint, this vast space is a retro paradise packed with vintage furniture, antique paraphernalia, and some of the best bric-a-brac around, from delightfully camp and kitsch to downright collectible.

Whether you're into collecting or not, this ever-changing treasure trove is the place to try your luck or enjoy browsing. The store owner—yes, there really is a Miss Pixie—sources her hauls from auctions, and she gets fresh stock in weekly, so locals check in regularly for new finds. Some items are unwieldy, but greeting cards, seashells, salt-and-pepper shakers, photo frames—these and more are all small enough to fit into your suitcase.

Salt & Sundry

Home and concept goodies that are great for gifts.

1625 14th Street NW

shopsaltandsundry.com

Mon–Sun 11am–6pm

Be warned: If your taste runs to boho-chic, this is the kind of place you walk into thinking, "I have carry-on only, so I'll just have a browse…" and before you know it, you're considering buying and checking an extra bag. This lovely, lovingly curated lifestyle boutique stocks, among other things, gorgeous colored glassware for entertaining, classy-with-a-touch-of-hippie cushions, and cozy throws for snuggling on the sofa. The owner led a previous life as a food journalist, so there's also a wonderful cookbook collection, as well as selected condiments and other ingredients.

Nifty gifts are sourced from all around the US, and new objects appear regularly. The original location is in Union Market, but this equally delightful branch is convenient for those in the area.

East City Bookshop

*Fabulous community-focused indie bookstore
in the heart of Capitol Hill.*

Brightly colored murals alert you to this otherwise unassuming place hidden in a basement on Pennsylvania Avenue (note: stair access only). Wander through its vibrant rooms, where the curation of books resembles an art gallery, and settle in to a relaxing reading nook. A regular program of book launches and readings pulls in the crowds.

Laurie Gillman, the passionate owner, is always up for a chat and recommendations. Since the bookstore's opening in 2016, she has worked hard to create a welcoming space, as reflected in the bookshelves; its many titles cater to kids, adults, the generally offbeat, LGBTQIA+ community, and a multitude of cultures and beliefs. I love the colorful, handwritten cards pinned to the shelves, sharing staff and customer reviews; it's all so deliciously bookish and oozes reading passion. (Oh, and don't miss the canine "customer" pics on the wall; yes, it's a dog-friendly operation).

If you're not in the market for books, browse the range of tempting gifts: puzzles, candles, socks, and journals, all literature-themed, of course.

---

645 Pennsylvania
Avenue SE

W
eastcitybookshop.com

Mon–Fri 11am–7pm
Sat 10am–7pm
Sun 11am–6pm

The Outrage

Fashion meets activism at this uncommon shop full of progressive messaging.

1811 14th Street NW

W

the-outrage.com

Mon–Thurs 9am–8pm
Fri & Sat 10am–8pm
Sun 10am–6pm

Since Washington, DC, is the hotbed of politics and lobbyists, home to the President and the US Congress, it's no wonder that folks around here are well, opinionated. These opinions seldom show up in DC's shops, though, as most of them tend toward the mainstream. One notable exception: The Outrage, which began as a pop-up shop for the Women's March in 2017. Now it's a full-time store that stocks everything the left-leaning voter needs to wear their heart on their sleeve. (Literally: Check the Ruth Bader Ginsberg hoodie with "May her memory be a revolution" printed down the arm.) Stock changes according to the issues of the day, but you may also find AOC action figures, onesies that read "squash the patriarchy," and tank tops with Angela Davis quotes.

The commercialism is backed up by activism, as the shop donates all profits to groups working for social change, and the shop doubles as a meeting space for political organizing and more.

GoodWood

Original high-quality, well-priced, bohemian-chic housewares and gifts.

1428 U Street NW

goodwooddc.com

Mon–Sun 12–6pm

GoodWood owners Anna and Dan Kahoe have a reputation for eclectic and inventive style; they could probably throw garbage together and make it look good. Opened in the 1990s, their shop was one of the first outposts of cool on U Street, a strip that later became known for retro goods and stores with unusual inventory. The other stores have come and gone—but GoodWood has stayed.

The store's quirky secondhand inventory comes from auctions and estate sales. You'll find everything from hefty sofas to smaller housewares and textiles. Quality is very high, and prices are oh so reasonable. Increasingly, however, I note that their range of clothing, soaps, and jewelry is expanding, so these days, it's more about the gifts than big-ticket midcentury pieces.

Solid State Books

*One of DC's best
independent bookstores.*

600 H Street NE

W

solidstatebooksdc.com

Mon–Sun 10am–8pm

If your vision of the ideal bookshop includes space and light, this is your nirvana. Airy and modern and plenty big, the space feels like a perfect antidote to summer heat and winter cold. As a partially Black-owned business, it stocks one of the city's most diverse selections of fiction and nonfiction titles, from airplane reads to meatier, political brain food. Plus it has a truly exciting children's section.

If you want to meet some of the H Street community, head here when there's an author reading or another event, such as local panel discussions or political conversations. These take place several times a week; check out the schedule on the website. Good Wi-Fi and nooks for reading encourage hanging out, and yes, there's even an aroma of coffee, thanks to its drip coffee on hand (though true aficionados might prefer an espresso drink from next door at The Wydown Coffee Shop; see p.56).

La Cosecha

Vivid textures, colors, and flavors at a chic Latino-themed market.

1280 4th Street NE

W

lacosechadc.com

Sun–Wed 8am–9pm
Thurs–Sat 8am–10pm

A relatively new addition to the Union Market District, La Cosecha ("the harvest") celebrates all things Latin American. The design is contemporary and chic, with a pleasant open-plan courtyard surrounded by store spaces. As of 2022, the market was still getting rolling, with a dozen or so vendors, from beautiful boutiques to a taqueria.

Uncover handmade jewelry, art, and baskets made by Venezuelan artisans at ArtTepuy; browse Brazilian designer goods at Nova Bossa; and pack all your finds up in a Mexico-made leather bag from Quavaro. Feeling hunger pangs? Grab an empanada from Peruvian Brothers and coffee from Café Unido (see p.59), or a brunch from Zumo, or gourmet tacos from Las Gemelas—and finally, treat yourself to superb handmade Venezuelan chocolates from Arcay Chocolates.

Politics and Prose

Lots of prose (but definitely not all politics) at this welcoming, well-known bookstore.

1270 5th Street NE

W

politics-prose.com

Tues–Sat 10am–8pm

Sun 11am–7pm

Politics and Prose opened its first store on Connecticut Avenue NW in 1984 with two staff, the founders Carla Cohen and Barbara Meade. Ownership has since changed, and it now employees over 100 people across three stores—the original location, plus this branch near Union Market and another in District Wharf—but the philosophy remains: "to cultivate community and strengthen the common good through books, programs, and a respectful exchange of ideas."

And these are not mere words. As well as stocking a massive range of titles by authors from around the globe, P&P (as it's affectionately known) also runs a prolific literary program at all three stores. Evening author talks are part of a local's routine; consult the online events calendar.

The branch in Union Market District is a cozy, modern space where it's pleasant to browse the ever-changing selection of hardback new releases, paperback fiction, and other nonfiction titles. It's conveniently next to The Village DC (see p.61).

Steadfast Supply

Stunning design store that supports independent brands and designers.

301 Tinegy Street SE

W

steadfastsupplydc.com

Tues–Fri 11am–7pm
Sat 10am–7pm
Sun 10am–6pm

An award-winning artist with Peruvian heritage, Virginia Arrisueño created Steadfast Supply as a pop-up shop in 2016 before opening this vibrant space in Navy Yard in 2019. Arrisueño, who grew up in Maryland and previously worked as a fashion designer, aims to support independent brands and designers from across the globe and right in the District. You'll find scented candles from 228 Grant Street, a Black-owned company in Baltimore; cookbooks with titles like *How to Be a Vegan and Keep Your Friends*; and fair-trade beaded purses from India. Then there are cards, kids' accessories, clothes, graphic T-shirts, even items for your pooch. It's perfect for gifts or designer-chic souvenirs, such as T-shirts with "202" (the local area code) or "51st," a nod to the movement for DC statehood.

The airy space itself is worthy of an Oscar for contemporary set design, with bright umbrellas, Chinese lanterns, and paper flowers hanging from the ceiling, and shelves and tables popping with brightly hued books, cushions, and hand-printed maps.

Capitol Hill Books

*This famous used bookstore rewards browsers
willing to dig.*

Opened in 1991, this historic row house has been accumulating odd books—and loyal customers—ever since. Now it is three floors of tomes devoted to every possible subject. And the subject labels, most written by longtime owner Jim Toole, are as fun to read as the books: "Coffee, tea, this, that and Juicing" is in the food section, appropriately in the house's former kitchen. "Hoity-toity books"—signed and first editions and rare books—are distinct from "Neither hoit nor toit." My favorite? The "Foreign Language Room," a narrow bookshelf wedged in the bathroom—not an insult to the French, German, and Spanish texts, but an expression of Toole's annoyance with inadequate American foreign-language education (it's "down the toilet," see?).

The organized chaos is a joy to meander through, especially if you're open to a serendipitous discovery. Though you hardly meander. More like wedge into whatever aisle is free of other bookworms—especially on weekends, when locals combine a visit to the farmers market across the street with a leisurely browse here.

In 2018, Toole, under pressure from property taxes and Amazon, wanted to retire and close the store. But a team of employees pooled resources to buy the place, and their enthusiasm and passion have kept the place open. And Toole still does a shift or two.

657 C Street SE   capitolhillbooks-dc.com   Mon–Fri 10am–8pm
Sat 9am–8pm
Sun 9am–7pm

DAY TRIP:
ALEXANDRIA, VIRGINIA

The old town of Alexandria, established in 1749, features some gorgeous row houses and historic homes, a packed commercial mile, and a revamped riverfront. Although very beautiful, it has a complicated past, as one of the country's main slave trading ports, and an interesting new museum addresses this. This circuit ticks off history, local cuisine, and shopping in half a day, or longer if you prefer. In summer, go by boat, and time your return for sunset views.

You'll arrive on a pier at the southeast side of town. From there, head straight to the **Torpedo Factory Art Center** and browse the three floors of artists' open studios. Five blocks away, peek into Prince Street, where the first pretty cobblestone block is known as **Captains Row**, after Captain John Harper, who built many of the strip's row homes in the 1700s.

Take Union Street south to **Café du Soleil**, a local favorite, for a light lunch of crêpes or a croque monsieur, then head back to Prince Street and turn left. At the next corner is **The Athenaeum**, an unmissable pink-stucco neoclassical building. Turn right on Lee Street; two blocks north, the cooperative Intertribal Creatives sells work by Native artisans from around North America. On nearby Royal Street, you can browse the well-curated **Old Town Books**, in a historic corner house.

Head west to Duke, where you'll find **Freedom House Museum**, in the 19th-century headquarters of the largest domestic slave-trafficking firm in the US, which sold and imprisoned thousands of men, women, and children here. The renovated museum, reopened in 2022, tells this story.

Keep an eye out for the Big Boy statue on South Payne Street: That's local institution **Goodies**, a '50s-look soda fountain with excellent Wisconsin-style frozen custard.

Continue north on Payne to King Street and turn right (east). On the left, **Made in Virginia** deals in stylish gifts by local designers. Two blocks ahead, eco-minded dry-goods store **Mason & Greens** also has excellent bakery items.

To return to the waterfront, catch the free King Street Trolley or walk a bit less than a mile (1.3km). At the water, head two blocks south to **Barca Pier & Wine Bar**, to enjoy a meal or a drink before your water taxi takes you back up the Potomac.

GETTING THERE

March to December, catch the Potomac Riverboat Company water taxi (cityexperiences.com/washington-dc) from Georgetown Waterfront (50 minutes) or District Wharf (30 minutes).

Otherwise, take the Metro (Yellow and Blue lines) to the King St-Old Town stop, on the west edge of the historic area. From here, a free trolley (visitalexandria.com/plan/king-street-trolley) runs every 15 minutes along the length of King Street to the Potomac, stopping every two to three blocks en route.

Day Trip

DAY TRIP:
GETTYSBURG, PENNSYLVANIA

Gettysburg, Pennsylvania, is a name synonymous with the American Civil War (1861–65), first due to a gruesome three-day battle that took place here in 1863, then for President Abraham Lincoln's famous speech, delivered five months later on what had become a cemetery. The Gettysburg Address, in which Lincoln encouraged the Union troops to fight on in the cause of preserving the young nation and its ethos of freedom, is engraved on the walls of the Lincoln Memorial in Washington, DC (see p.156).

These days, visitors can tour the former battle site, and a fascinating visitor center, while the nearby town of Gettysburg offers historic buildings, excellent foodie choices, and a great sense of its important legacy.

Head first to the **Gettysburg National Military Park Museum & Visitor Center** (nps.gov/gett) for an orientation. Twelve galleries cover the period before, during, and after the Civil War. But it's the Gettysburg Cyclorama, an extraordinary, giant 360-degree painting of the battle made in 1884, accompanied by a narration of the key events, that really puts you in the middle of the action, in every sense.

Afterward, get an early lunch in town: A jumbo sandwich pairs with a craft brew at **Appalachian Brewing Company**, or get your teeth into a quiche and other baked goods from **Gettysburg Baking Company**. Then return to the visitor center for a 3.5-hour guided bike tour around the battlefield with **GettysBike Tours**. (You could also go on horseback, or simply in your own car with a map from the visitor center.)

In late afternoon, check out one of the in-town museums, **Shriver House Museum** or **Jennie Wade House**, both of which reveal what happened to the homes' occupants during the Confederate incursion. Throw back a predinner pint at **Garryowen Irish Pub** (it also stocks over 100 varieties of Irish whiskey) before enjoying a local bite. For those who want to continue the historic theme, **Dobbin House**, a historic tavern that opened in 1776, has you covered. If you prefer to reenter contemporary society, try the range of brick-oven pizzas and scrumptious modern American fare at **Mela Kitchen**.

GETTING THERE

Located 78 miles (125km) north of Washington, DC, Gettysburg is best accessed by car. Alternatively, Amtrak trains run from DC's Union Station to Harrisburg, PA; from there, catch a Rabbit Express connector bus. These are weekday commuter buses, however, so the schedule is limited.

If you don't know much about George Washington, America's first president, visit Mount Vernon, and you'll be fit to lead the country—or at least give a school report on George—by the time you leave. In a day outing to his historic estate, you'll get fascinating insight into the Washington family's life, an immersion that covers a lot more than mere politics.

Mount Vernon (mountvernon.org) was Washington's home estate, an elegant 21-room house surrounded by lush gardens and farmland. The whole space is maintained as much more than a typical historic-mansion tour.

On the farm, for instance, costumed interpreters demonstrate farming practices used on the plantation, mostly by enslaved people. (Washington owned 123 people, and although the Mount Vernon official history doesn't shy away from this fact, it does take pains to say that in his will, Washington specified that on the death of his wife, everyone would be freed.)

Wander up to the house, through orchards, flowerbeds, and sweeping lawns, to the museum and information center. The displays here, with scale models and films, fill in any knowledge gaps. Especially interesting are the family's personal items, such as clothing and furniture—and even George's dentures! (Contrary to legend, they were not made of wood; I won't spoil the surprise.) If you can, chat with "Martha Washington," who occasionally entertains visitors with snippets of gossip. It's testament to the interpreters' talents that such performances are not kitschy, but genuinely informative. Then it's back to reality: Pay homage to the former president and first lady at their tomb, located south of the fruit garden and nursery.

The one weak spot is the cafeteria, which sells uninspiring junk food; the Mount Vernon Inn Restaurant, also on the grounds, is preferable but more expensive. Unfortunately, picnics are not permitted on the estate.

Weekends and public holidays can get a bit busy, though this is when you're guaranteed to have interpreters in character. (If this is one of your reasons for coming, check for "Character Conversations" in the calendar on the website.) But if you arrive early, you'll have the place to yourself for a bit. To smell Washington's roses. Literally.

GETTING THERE
Mount Vernon is about 15 miles (25km) southwest of Washington, DC. Public transit takes about 1.5 hours: Take the Metro Yellow line to Huntington; here, change to a Fairfax connector bus 101 (fairfaxcounty.gov/connector; one to two per hour). Keen cyclists can follow a designated bike trail from downtown DC (allow around two hours).

DAY TRIP:
RICHMOND, VIRGINIA

Richmond, Virginia, long known primarily for its slave trade and as the onetime capital of the Confederacy, has recently begun to reexamine its history. Between some fabulous museums and hip foodie spots, gorgeous gardens, and tree-lined streets, you can make a fascinating day out. Given the city's distance from DC, though, it's worth staying overnight if you can.

Start in the Carytown neighborhood, 2 miles (3.2km) west of the center. West Cary Street is an enticing strip of vintage clothing boutiques and the retro **Byrd Theater**. Grab a snack at **Sugar & Twine**, a from-scratch bakery, or for a quick lunch, head to nearby **Roastology**, housed in a former gas station. It's now one of the city's many excellent coffee spots and serves scrumptious sandwiches. Also good for coffee is **Blanchards** on Morris Street, while **Sub Rosa** in Church Hill serves great brews along with some of the best baked goods in the US. From here, walk to the **Virginia Museum of Fine Arts**, where the collection runs from contemporary American artists to European modernism. Wander north to Monument Avenue, once lined with statues of Confederate leaders like Robert E. Lee; after years of protest, all five were removed in 2020 and 2021, along with six other statues in the city. Remaining: the **Arthur Ashe Monument**, in a traffic circle at Roseneath Road, honoring the Black tennis player, a hometown hero.

Next stop is **downtown Richmond**, where on the banks of the **James River** once stood Shockoe Bottom, a vast infrastructure for selling human beings, second only in size to New Orleans' slave market. All traces are gone, but you can learn more about the slave trade at the revamped **American Civil War Museum**, which aims to tell the story of the war from the perspective of enslaved people, Confederates, and Unionists—though some visitors have noted they are not evenly weighted. Wander east along the river to **The Poe Museum** and commune with the ghost of Edgar Allan himself, who grew up in Richmond in the 1810s. By late afternoon, the galleries of the **Downtown Arts District** come to life. Veer north into **Jackson Ward**, designated the Black neighborhood since the 1870s, when the city council gerrymandered the area to restrict the voting influence of recently freed people.

For dinner, head east to Church Hill, where **Alewife** serves fresh and creative seafood, or to **Scott's Addition**, to hop between craft breweries. For hotels? Consider the traditional **Linden Row Inn** or arty, minimalist **Quirk Hotel**.

GETTING THERE

Richmond is approximately 100 miles (160km) south from Washington, DC. Amtrak trains (three daily) from Union station take a little under three hours. Flixbus (global.flixbus.com) and Megabus (us.megabus.com) have daily services. Driving, I-95 takes you directly to Richmond in about 2.5 hours, but if you have time, take more scenic Route 1 (about four hours).

Day Trip

THE ESSENTIALS

DC is a well-organized city and, once you grasp that a couple of large diagonal streets distract you from an otherwise perfect grid, it's easy to find your way around. Whether you're a first-time visitor or you're back for more, these tips will help you hit the streets like a local.

GETTING TO/FROM WASHINGTON, DC

Plane

DC has two airports. Ronald Reagan Airport (DCA) handles domestic flights plus some flights to/from Canada. It's definitely the easier airport to navigate, and only 4 miles (6.5km) from downtown, about 45 minutes on the Metro (Yellow and Blue lines) or a 20-minute cab ride.

Washington Dulles (IAD) is the city's international flight hub, in Virginia, 26 miles (42km) from DC. The new-in-2022 Silver line Metro connects to Union Station in 64 minutes; Metro Center (53 minutes) is another useful stop. Other options include taking a cab (Washington Flyer) or a rideshare service.

Train

The beautiful Beaux-Arts Union Station (unionstationdc.com; 50 Massachusetts Ave NE) has intercity trains, plus a Metro stop (Red line).

Amtrak (amtrak.com) links East Coast cities with its Northeast Regional and marginally faster Acela services. MARC (Maryland Rail Commuter; mta.maryland.gov) serves Baltimore and other smaller Maryland towns.

Bus

Buses regularly ply the route between DC and New York. With heavy competition, they are by far the cheapest way between cities, but they can be delayed by traffic. Washington Deluxe (866-287-6932, washny.com) is one of many options; its coaches depart from a handy location in Dupont Circle.

GETTING AROUND WASHINGTON, DC

On Foot

With its generally flat topography and orderly street grid, DC is an extremely walkable city. The city blocks are large, however, and distances can be deceptive. The Mall alone is 2.2 miles (3.5km) long. Excellent walking tour companies include DC Insider Tours

THE ESSENTIALS

(dcinsidertours.com) and Free Tours by Foot (freetoursbyfoot.com).

Bus

Metrobus (wmata.com) operates throughout the DC metro area. Useful Circulator buses (dccirculator.com) cover downtown and the central neighborhoods. The National Mall route is particularly handy, as it goes between major monuments along the Mall and around the Tidal Basin. Tourist buses, including the double-decker Big Bus, allow you to hop on and off. These are well worth considering if you're sightseeing rather than heading to a particular street location.

Metro

The Washington Metro (wmata.com) connects all four quadrants of DC proper, as well as parts of Virginia and Maryland. Commuters gripe about inefficiencies, but it works well around the center. Fares are based on the number of stops traveled; prices are reasonable, but steeper in morning and evening rush hours.

Paying for Transit

Buses take cash (pay at the front in exact change only), and individual Metro tickets can be purchased from machines in stations. But it's far easier to pay on both buses and trains with the SmarTrip phone app, or with a rechargeable SmarTrip card. You can buy the cards with cash or credit at any Metro station or in advance on wmata.com. Load the card with credit, then tap at gates on entry and exit. On buses, tap by the driver only as you board, not when you leave.

Bike

DC has a number of bike lanes and flat terrain, but drivers are not very bike aware, and traffic moves fast. Children under 16 are required by law to wear a helmet.

Capital Bikeshare (capitalbikeshare .com; 877-430-BIKE) has many stations throughout the city. Day passes (S8) allow unlimited use of bikes for 24 hours. To avoid additional fees, keep each ride under 45 minutes; this may require docking your bike mid-trip and taking a new one. The bikes are especially useful for getting around the Mall, though docks can fill up. If you run into problems, calling the support number can work better than using the app; staff can extend your time limit while you look for an open dock, for instance.

Taxi and App-Based Rides

Cabs can be hailed in the street or outside major hotels. Uber and Lyft are also available, but are not necessarily cheaper than taxis; taxis are usually better for shorter distances. Alternatively, the apps Curb and DC Yellow Cab offer app convenience for taxis, but prices may be slightly higher than the meter rate.

Water Taxi

From March to December, boats (cityexperiences.com/washington-dc) connect District Wharf, Georgetown, Old Town Alexandria (Virginia), and National Harbor (Maryland). Prices include an audio tour, so it's more for tourists than daily commuters, but it is an enjoyable way to see vistas of the nation's capital from the Potomac.

Car

You won't have much need for a car if you're sticking to the downtown area, or the neighborhoods within this book. Parking is not too difficult, though, with many large parking lots and garages around the center. Generally, the nearer a major sight, the more parking will cost. On the street, meters take credit cards, and some take coins. Note that you cannot park along the Mall, but there are parking garages within a block of key museums.

Traffic can be heavy, especially at peak commuting hours in the morning and evening (when traffic flow on major arteries can change direction; be alert to signs). Traffic circles are also common, though those downtown tend to have traffic lights; if not, yield to traffic coming from the left (in the circle). DC drivers tend to err on the side of speed (despite a limit in residential neighborhoods of 20mph/32kmph) and often do not use their turn signals. On the Capital Beltway (I-495), left-lane exits are not uncommon; look out for surprised drivers veering suddenly toward them.

Driving Tips for International Visitors

International visitors can drive a car or motorcycle with a full and valid license for three months after entry to the US. To hire a car, you'll need a license with a photograph. Renting a car is common, and companies include Avis, Budget, and National. Read the fine print on insurance; in DC and Virginia, the rental agency is required to provide liability insurance (to cover damage to third parties); your credit card may provide collision insurance (covering the damage you might do to the car). Many agencies charge a fee for drivers younger than 25.

Seatbelts are mandatory. On multilane roads and highways, drive primarily in the right lane(s) and use the left (driver's side) only for passing (overtaking); avoid passing on the right. Within DC, it is legal to turn right on a red light, unless signs state otherwise, but as of 2022, this law was being reconsidered, so double-check with your rental agency.

EATING AND DRINKING IN WASHINGTON, DC

Restaurant Reservations

For anything beyond informal cafés, it's well worth reserving a table, usually done through online services such as Resy and OpenTable. For formal places, this should definitely be done a week or two ahead. That said, if you arrive just after opening time, first-come-first-served bar seating is often available.

Tipping

Tipping is embedded in American culture; restaurant and bar workers are paid substantially less than the (already low) minimum wage and rely on tips to make up the difference. As of 2022, a new law in DC will phase out this practice and bring service workers up to full minimum wage by 2027. How this will affect tipping culture in the long run is unclear, but in the meantime, get in the habit of factoring in tips. For sit-down meals, add between 15 and 25 percent of the pretax amount; at a bar, add $1 or $2 per drink. In places with counter service only, such as coffee bars, tipping conventions are less rigid; regulars often do tip their baristas, though.

Tip at hotels as well: luggage porters, room service, and housekeeping should all receive $2 to $5 at the time of service (or, with housekeeping, per guest per day).

SPECIAL EVENTS

Cherry Blossom Festival

Several weeks in late March and early April celebrate the peak blooms of the capital's cherry trees, a gift presented in 1912 by the mayor of Tokyo.

Photographers cram the Tidal Basin, and there's a parade, themed art installations, and even blossom-themed cocktails and meals (nationalcherryblossomfestival.org).

DC Jazz Festival

Dates vary for this summer fest (dcjazzfest.org), but it's usually a packed five days or so with top American and international jazz artists in venues around the city; some shows are free.

Pride Month

To celebrate DC's dynamic LGBTQIA+ community, each June, Capital Pride (capitalpride.org) hosts a week's worth of events, including a parade, a festival, and a big concert. It's not exactly Brazilian Mardi Gras, but it's fun all the same. Black Pride (dcblackpride.org) usually kicks off Pride Month, starting with events over Memorial Day weekend, at the end of May.

Independence Day

On July 4, head to the Mall—along with seemingly everyone else in the city—to watch the fireworks burst over the Washington Monument. Oddly, the show itself is not so spectacular (depending on your view); it's more about the symbolism than the bang.

Smithsonian Folklife Festival

For around 10 days near July 4, this celebration (festival.si.edu) embraces folkloric customs from all around the world through activities, concerts, and interactive displays.

Public Holidays

Public galleries, Smithsonian museums, and anything related to the government closes for holidays, but many businesses are open.

Martin Luther King Day – third Monday in January
Presidents Day – third Monday in February
Emancipation Day (DC) – April 16 or nearest weekday
Memorial Day – last Monday in May
Juneteenth – June 19 or nearest weekday
Independence Day – July 4 (and nearest Monday or Friday, if it falls on a weekend)
Labor Day – first Monday in September
Thanksgiving Day – fourth Thursday in November
Veterans Day – November 11
Christmas Day - December 25 (and nearest Monday or Friday, if on weekend)

PRACTICALITIES

Media and Tourist Information
Destination DC (washington.org): official info from the Washington, DC, visitor organization.

The Washingtonian (washingtonian. com): The website of this monthly magazine is a useful source of local snippets on restaurants, galleries, and more. Often features interviews with high-flying locals, from lobbyists to chefs.

Eater DC (dc.eater.com): ever-changing curation of the latest foodie spots, plus themed ideas.

Time Zone
Washington, DC, is on Eastern Standard Time (EST), five hours behind Greenwich Mean Time. Eastern Daylight Time begins in mid-March and ends at the start of November (usually one week before and after the change in Europe).

Money and ATMs
Banks seem to occupy every corner in DC. Some stores and corners have standalone ATMs, though it's recommended to use those located on bank premises in case you have a problem with your card. If using a foreign card, make sure the ATM displays one of the international symbols—Plus, Interac, Maestro, or Cirrus. You'll probably be charged a usage fee (by your home bank) for using a foreign ATM. Note for Australians and New Zealanders: Many ATMs require you to select withdrawal from either "checking" or "savings," so be sure to know which type your account is considered. Digital wallets are widely accepted, but if not, credit cards are accepted in most DC locations. Nevertheless, it's handy to carry cash, especially dollar bills, for tips.

Climate
DC may be relatively far south, but it is not exempt from extreme weather: snow and ice and bitter cold in winter and, conversely, brutal humidity and heat in summer. Between June and August, temperatures average 80°F (27°C), though it can hit 95°F (35°C), with 70 percent humidity.

Phone and Internet
US phone carriers use either GSM or CDMA systems. International visitors wanting to use their smartphones can purchase prepaid SIM cards from AT&T or T-Mobile, assuming your phone is GSM-compatible. For phone calls only, you can buy prepaid cards from convenience stores (including Best Buy and Walmart) and pharmacies to make local, long-distance, and overseas calls.

If you don't feel like spending on a US SIM card, or paying international roaming fees (check what overseas plans your provider offers), or want to squeak by with a small data plan, you can just about get around on the free Wi-Fi in many cafés, bars, hotels, museums, and tourist attractions.

Voltage and converters

US appliances are fitted with plugs that have either two rectangular pins or a triangle of pins, two rectangular and one round. Voltage is 120 V, 60 Hz, so be aware you can't use hairdryers and shavers from countries with the more standard 220/240 AC voltage.

Safety

While most of downtown DC and surrounding neighborhoods are generally safe, and visitors are not targets of any particular crime, take care in the evenings, especially around H Street and Shaw/U Street Corridors, where incidents of gun violence have occurred.

LGBTQIA+ Travelers

DC has a thriving community and, thanks to its many queer-oriented establishments and activities, it ranks as one of America's most gay-friendly cities. Dupont Circle, Logan Circle (especially 17th and U Streets), and 14th Street are the hearts of gay life. Of the various useful websites, start with Capital Pride (capitalpride.org), DC Black Pride (dcblackpride.org), and Destination DC's listings (washington.org/lgbtq).

Travelers with Disabilities

Trains and buses are wheelchair accessible. All DC Metro stations have elevators (though they're not always working). Unfortunately onboard PA systems announcing forthcoming stations are appallingly hard to hear. By law, guide dogs are permitted to accompany you everywhere.

For wheelchair users, your main annoyances are buckled sidewalks, particularly in the historic areas of Capitol Hill and Georgetown. Downtown, sidewalks are generally in good condition, with curb cuts (access points). Street crossings have audio signals.

All Smithsonian museums have tours for hearing-impaired visitors, as well as free wheelchair loans (si.edu/visit/visitorswithdisabilities).

THE ESSENTIALS

Photo credits

All images ã Kate Armstrong except for the following:

Front cover: Chris Fukuda Photography; Pages ii-iii Andy Feliciotti/Unsplash; 2 Colby Ray/Unsplash; 25 David Harmantas / Shutterstock.com; 28; 30 The Jefferson; 34 Cate Brown; 36 The Fainting Goat; 38 Lia Manfredi; 45 luestone Lane; 42, 49 Grace Street Coffee; 53 Rey Lopez; 66 Dirty Habit; 67 Off the Record; 68 Washington Hotel; 75 Emilio Pabon Photography; 79 STREETSENSE; 87 Lulu's; 95 Last Call; 100, 157, 214 courtesy of washington.org; 102 Courtesy of Restaurant Associates; 103 Greg Powers Photography; 104 Carmine's; 110 Shimon Tammara; 113 (top) Call Your Mother; 119 Chiko; 120 Emissary; 127 Compass Rose; 129 Le Diplomate; 135 The Royal; 137 Supra; 144 The District Fishwife; 145 Jennifer Chase; 152 David Trinks/Unsplash; 154 Matailong Du; 155 Library of Congress; 158 National Gallery of Art; 168, 171 courtesy of The Wharf; 174 Artechouse; 179 Planet Word; 182 Alamy Photos; 183 John Shore; 200 Laura Metzler Photography; 202 Bruce Guthrie; 203 Emma McAlary; 206 Kristian Summerer for Visit Alexandria.

The Essentials

THANK YOU

A huge shout-out to Megan Cuthbert and Melissa Kayser for giving me the opportunity to get my teeth into this amazing city and to work with Hardie Grant.

In DC, thanks to Julie Marshall of Destination DC, who, despite the pandemic blip, was able to help me pick up the trail; DC geeks Ali and Sajay, for pointing me in the right directions; Sarah Crozier, for her barhopping skills and knowledge of the cocktail scene; and Katie Meyers, for her last-minute assistance. Also to Chris for his patience and orientation, and for helping me polish off ridiculously massive numbers of dishes, cocktails, and more. And a huge shout out to Penny Watson for her generous introduction to the HG stable, and to Edie for her camera skills.

Finally, to Zora O'Neill, an extraordinary editor who not only polished the text but queried, debated, and clarified all-important American details—thank you.

Kate Armstrong is an award winning travel writer whose work is published regularly across the globe. Over the past 17 years, she's notched up scores of Lonely Planet guides and coffee-table titles. Unearthing quirky aspects of a city and country is Kate's 'thing' – she loves chatting, eating, drinking and dancing her way into cultures. For the last decade she's been based in and out of Washington, DC and has thrived on the city's cuisine renaissance cultural scene. Find out more at katearmstrongtravelwriter.com and on Instagram @nomaditis.

Published in 2023 by Hardie Grant Explore,
an imprint of Hardie Grant Publishing

Hardie Grant Explore (Melbourne)
Wurundjeri Country
Building 1, 658 Church Street
Richmond, Victoria 3121

Hardie Grant Explore (Sydney)
Gadigal Country
Level 7, 45 Jones Street
Ultimo, NSW 2007

www.hardiegrant.com/au/explore

The maps in this publication incorporate data from
OpenStreetMap www.openstreetmap.org/copyright

OpenStreetMap is open data, licensed under the
Open Data Commons Open Database License
(ODbL) by the OpenStreetMap Foundation (OSMF).
https://opendatacommons.org/licenses/odbl/1-0/

Any rights in individual contents of the database
are licensed under the Database Contents
License: https://opendatacommons.org/licenses/
dbcl/1-0/

Data extracts via Geofabrik GmbH https://www.
geofabrik.de

A catalogue record for this
book is available from the
National Library of Australia

Hardie Grant acknowledges the Traditional
Owners of the Country on which we work, the
Wurundjeri People of the Kulin Nation and the
Gadigal People of the Eora Nation, and recognises
their continuing connection to the land, waters
and culture. We pay our respects to their Elders
past and present.

Beyond the Monuments in Washington, D.C.
ISBN 9781741177169

10 9 8 7 6 5 4 3 2 1

Project editor
Megan Cuthbert
Editor
Zora O'Neill
Proofreader
Collin Vogt
Cartographer
Claire Johnston
Design
Muse Muse
Typesetting
Hannah Schubert

Colour reproduction by Hannah Schubert
and Splitting Image Colour Studio

Printed and bound in China by LEO Paper
Products LTD.

The paper this book is printed on is
certified against the Forest
Stewardship Council® Standards
and other sources. FSC® promotes
environmentally responsible, socially
beneficial and economically viable
management of the world's forests.

Disclaimer: While every care is taken to
ensure the accuracy of the data within this
product, the owners of the data do not make
any representations or warranties about its
accuracy, reliability, completeness or suitability
for any particular purpose and, to the extent
permitted by law, the owners of the data disclaim
all responsibility and all liability (including
without limitation, liability in negligence) for all
expenses, losses, damages (including indirect
or consequential damages) and costs which
might be incurred as a result of the data being
inaccurate or incomplete in any way and for
any reason.

Publisher's Disclaimers: The publisher cannot
accept responsibility for any errors or omissions.
The representation on the maps of any road or
track is not necessarily evidence of public right of
way. The publisher cannot be held responsible for
any injury, loss or damage incurred during travel.
It is vital to research any proposed trip thoroughly
and seek the advice of relevant state and travel
organisations before you leave.

Publisher's Note: Every effort has been made
to ensure that the information in this book
is accurate at the time of going to press. The
publisher welcomes information and suggestions
for correction or improvement.